A New Creation
Giving Hope in a Hopeless World
~Missy Denard~

"Therefore if any man be in Christ, he is a new creature: old things are passed away; behold, all things are become new."
2 Corinthians 5:17
(KJV)

A NEW
CREATION

MISSY DENARD

Cover Design: Carly Tobias
Cover Image: Anya Kubilus
Author's Photograph: Catherine Cisneros

HV Chapman & Sons
PO Box 111
Abilene, Texas 79604

New Beginnings – Big Country
P.O. Box 4193
Abilene, Texas 79608

ISBN: 978-1-940850-12-2

Dedication

To my loving, patient husband, Rocky for enduring all the time it takes for the ministry to help so many women; and also for never complaining of not having dinner, but supporting me to follow what God has called me to do. God has used you to show me what real love is, and I'm so thankful He gave you to me!

Acknowledgments

Sometimes in life, God calls us to do the "impossible". That was my first response when He told me I was supposed to write a book about my life story. Never in my wildest dreams did I think I would be writing a book, but He put some key people in my life to help make this a reality.

First of all, I want to give all glory to my Lord and Savior, Jesus Christ for making this possible.

I would like to especially thank my sister-in-law, Leigh Denard Little and her husband Steve, who was so understanding to let me take Leigh away from their family business and to free her up to spend countless hours editing this book. Leigh felt led to help me, and with her background in English and a Masters in Education, I felt that she was a God sent gift. She helped me pour over two years of notes I'd made plus poems, testimonies and letters that the women had given me over the years. I love her more than words can say, she is so beautiful inside and out. She was so dedicated to getting the book done so others could be encouraged by what Jesus has done in my life as well as in so many others.
Leigh, you truly are my sister in Christ, and I love you very,very, much!

Missy Denard

Acknowledgments

Thank you to Ms. Wanda Murphree for spurring me on to write this book and for praying me through. Although this project took longer to complete, as we know, it's all in His perfect timing!

A special thank you to Carly Tobias for all she poured into our ministry by donating her time, efforts and talents as graphic designer designing our book cover.

Also a special thank you to Jo Denard, my mother-in-law for volunteering her time after retiring from 30 years of teaching to keep the administrative part of New Beginnings flowing. I appreciate her taking on such a task as this! And a big thank you to Al Denard, my father-in-law for putting up with me and loving me no matter what!

Last, but definitely not least, a big thank you to all the volunteers who have served in the past and those presently serving whether seen on a regular basis or those who serve a more "behind the scenes" kind of role, we couldn't do what we do without you! We are also appreciative and thankful for our supporters and prayer partners. You are all equally valuable to our ministry!

Contents

Foreword by Larry Goff.............................. 1

Introduction.. 3

Chapter 1 Beauty For Ashes 5

Chapter 2 Jail Ministry 23

Chapter 3 Ordained 29

Chapter 4 God's Touch 33

Chapter 5 New Beginnings 53

Chapter 6 Divine Intervention 70

Chapter 7 Three Years of Pain.................. .83

Chapter 8 Blessings Received................... 93

Chapter 9 Testimonies of Healing and Hope........... 99

Chapter 10 Poems … 159

Chapter 11 Letters................................. 181

Chapter 12 Call To Action… 207

Epilogue.. 209

Foreword

My wife, Betty and I first met Missy and her husband, Rocky at a home group meeting in Abilene, Texas. Almost immediately, we recognized that Missy had an anointing on her life and a calling from God. She and others from the home group began going out witnessing with me at night to seek the lost.

From this time on, God gave Missy a heart to help these people she came across, especially the women. Later, as her calling grew stronger, and based on my 50 years of ministry from when Jesus divinely ordered me to take the gospel into all the world, I felt led to ordain Missy for ministry. It was so obvious to me that God had ordained Missy to demonstrate His loving compassion for rejected and unlovable people. Therefore, in front of many witnesses, along with her husband, I confirmed what God had already ordained. It was unusual in the eyes of men to see a woman ordained to minister the gospel of Jesus Christ.

In the Scriptures, I saw two women whom God had ordained to carry His word into the world. The first woman evangelist was the Samaritan woman at the well, who after leading a whole town to Jesus had obviously been filled with the true living water that He offered. The second woman was Mary Magdalene, who received a divine order from two angels at Christ's empty tomb to go tell His disciples that He had risen.

It is obvious to me, and all who are called of the Lord, that God will call His ministers, not according to gender, but according to His own choosing, no matter what the religious world thinks. It's so awesome to me to see Christ continue His ministry to the lost, homeless and hurting people through a vessel like Missy.

At this time, Missy started a woman's jail ministry; and a few years later, God put it on her heart to start a transitional home for women. That's how New Beginnings was born. Many women have been helped through this ministry, and God is going to reach many more women for the Lord Jesus Christ as this ministry continues.

Larry Goff, Goff Ministries

Introduction

I have been compelled to write this book ever since God put it on my heart just a short time ago while I was going through one of the most challenging times since giving my life to Jesus Christ. It just would not go away. The fact that somehow I had to tell my story about how God moved in my life before I even knew Him stayed with me. The more I thought about it, the more I knew He wanted to use my story to give hope to other women; and so they would know that the things He did for me, He would also do for them. I was reluctant to dive back into a painful past. Since many of the people in my life are changed as well, I did not want to recall the things that had caused hurt. I'm writing this as an act of obedience to God in hopes that my story will give women a ray of light when their world seems filled with darkness.

I realized that this urging was not going away. When Ms. Wanda, a volunteer, told me she was suppose to help me with my book, and I had not told anyone about my promptings from God, I knew I had to face my past and just do it. She got the ball rolling and encouraged me, and then pushed some more. I knew I would need a lot of help from friends and loved ones in order to pull this off.

It is so incredibly humbling to think that God would use me to help lost, broken and hurting women. He can turn our messes into His message for others. It's all about our intimate relationship with Jesus. It has never been about what I can do; it's about being obedient to what He tells me to do. It is all for His glory, not ours. It's priceless to me to see all the lives that are truly changed and transformed into new creations!

Chapter 1

Beauty for Ashes

"The Spirit of the Lord God is upon me, because the Lord has anointed me to preach good tidings to the poor: He has sent me to heal the brokenhearted, to proclaim liberty to the captives, and the opening of the prison to those who are bound: To proclaim the acceptable year of the Lord, and the day of vengeance of our God: to comfort all who mourn, to console those who mourn in Zion, To Give Them Beauty For Ashes, the oil of joy for mourning, the garment of praise for the spirit of heaviness." Isaiah 61:1-3a (NKJV)

~~~~~~~~~~~~~~~~~~~~

I was raised in a small Texas town as the only girl with three brothers in a highly dysfunctional family. However, I didn't realize just how dysfunctional we really were until I was much older. My father and mother were married and had two boys who were 18 months and 2 ½ years old when I was born.

My earliest childhood memory was running down the road at a young age to my grandmother's house crying because my daddy was beating up my mother because she had other men in our house. Their

3

marriage ended in divorce, and we (my two older brothers and I) stayed at my grandparents' house most of the time. My mother eventually re-married, and we had a step-dad who didn't have any children of his own; suddenly he had three of us. Their marriage produced another little boy who was the youngest by seven years. I became a tomboy, loving to play football, baseball, etc. with the boys, which made me very tough. My brothers and I fought all the time, and they loved to torment me. They would make scratching noises on my window at night or hide under my bed and grab my legs when I would go to get in bed. I was so scared that I couldn't sleep. This torment caused a deep-rooted fear in me. I was extremely scared of the dark. So scared that I would sleep in the bathroom with the door locked, the light on, and a towel rolled at the bottom so the light couldn't be seen from the hallway. I also had issues with bed-wetting that I would get beaten for from my mother and step dad. This was another reason I was afraid to sleep in my bed.

I grew up around lies and manipulation. I learned to mimic every trait. People I thought were safe abused me. From as early as I can remember, I was molested by family members. It didn't stop until I was thirteen years old. I was so confused about love that I thought it was sex. A close family friend raped me when I was 12 years old. A doctor confirmed this the next morning through tests; however, my mother never believed me and even took the friend's side denying anything had happened to me. Even though I know I wasn't, I felt ugly and fat, and experienced rejection, but never true love. This caused a very low self-esteem. I thought I could never be better, so "normal life" for me was not what one would call "normal".

My mother divorced again, and things only got worse. We never felt stability again. Even while I was being physically abused, those around me would also abuse me mentally and emotionally by saying, "You better not tell anything or you will be in more trouble." This made me feel ashamed and afraid. I trusted no one. Everyone I thought was trustworthy proved not to be.

By this time, my mother had gotten caught up in drugs. She spent a lot of time going to bars, drinking and doing drugs with different men and her friends. She took me with her to bars on numerous occasions where she would meet up with different men. I walked in on several occasions to find drugs on the table, and I even found drugs set up on the bathroom counter intended for her. When I was 13, my mother's boyfriend at the time introduced me to pot. It made me feel weird, and I didn't like it.

At age 14, my mother left the three of us (my two older brothers and me) alone in our apartment in the projects, so I went to live with my ex-stepdad so I could go to school. My younger brother still lived with him. I ended up quitting school the same year, which was my 8th grade year. My two older brothers were so determined to stay in school in order to play sports that they spent nights in someone's barn and showered at the school. Timmy excelled in pole vaulting, and Shannon was extremely fast and really good in football. Because of the lack of parental guidance, they both ended up in and out of jail as well as prison.

I then moved in with my dad and stepmother, and started working at a little restaurant called Ken's Chicken & Fish. I didn't like the rules at my dad's house, so I moved in with my grandparents...I was just kind of "everywhere"... trying to find a place where I fit in.

Then, things changed! I see it now as God's guiding hand. Ken's family became a very important part of my life, and they began to teach me the right way to live. They began to love me unconditionally, which stabilized the way I was living. Ken and Ellen started sowing seeds into my life. They taught me many things from work ethic to how to parallel park an extended cab, long bed Ford F-150 truck. They both went with me to take my driving test, and let me use their vehicle. Their son and daughter-in-law, Keith and Melinda also spent countless hours counseling me. Keith had begun preaching, so I attended his church at times. He poured the love of JESUS into my life by being a godly man and a true friend. Even in the midst of many mistakes I made, he was always there helping me and not judging. I looked up to him, and loved the whole family with all my heart. Later, he baptized me in Lake Hubbard.

I really didn't understand much at that time, as it was an emotional experience only; my life wasn't truly changed. I didn't want to disappoint these people who had shown me so much love. I was too embarrassed at the time to say I didn't understand. What I didn't know was that when Jesus truly comes into your life, you are FOREVER changed. It is finished and final at the moment you believe. I thought that being immersed in water would make me be like them. It was a seed planted in my heart, but not a true repentance. My life wasn't changed as I still did worldly things without conviction. Looking back, I know that God placed me there for a reason. We never know what fruit will be produced once a seed is planted. I'm one of them. I started busing tables, and in eight years I had worked my way up to being manager.

At age 16, a terrible tragedy happened in my life. A car wreck almost killed me. I was riding with a friend in a Ford Escort, and we hit the wheel of an eastbound 18 Wheeler on Interstate 20. We rolled across the median and into the westbound traffic sliding into the guardrail, which kept us from going into a creek full of water. I was thrown into the back seat, and a guardrail post came through the passenger window. But I remember a special lady came and picked me up, and sat me down on the guardrail. I was choking on my own blood and almost bit off my tongue. I had severe damage to my head, back, legs and neck. When the ambulance came I said, "Where's the lady who picked me up?" The reply was, "What lady? We're the first on the scene, and there was no lady." I truly believe she was an angel; her comforting voice kept assuring me I was going to be okay. I was in the hospital for over two weeks, and they wouldn't let me look in the mirror until after the first week. My situation was really bad, and I know I survived only by the Grace of God. I was living with my grandparents at the time of my accident, and I had lied about where I was going. I learned a very big lesson in that. I tried to contact and thank the lady through the local paper, but there was never a reply, which further led me to believe that this really was an angel that no one else saw.

I had been dating an older guy, and we were in love (at least by my definition of love); and I soon became pregnant. He was angry and begged me to have an abortion, but I was stubborn enough that I said, "No way; I'll make it on my own." However, I soon learned that I couldn't.

During this next chapter of my life, I moved in with my mother who was living in east Texas, and she helped me throughout the pregnancy. I was still searching for love, and as soon as the baby was born, I moved to Ranger, Texas to live with a different guy and his family. That didn't work out either, so I moved back to my daddy's house and started working at "Ken's" again. I started saving money so I could get my own apartment. I bought all my furnishings from garage sales, and then I was on my own. By this time, my little boy was over a year old.

Now I was a single mom at 17, and I was supporting the two of us. I tried very hard not to make the same mistakes I grew up with, but I still did. I started dating a man who was much older than I, and after we had been dating for a while, I found out that he was married. He told me they were separated, but that wasn't true. I got pregnant again and didn't want to have two kids without being married, so I had an abortion. It was horrific; no words can really describe it!

I started dating another guy when I was 19, and got pregnant once again. This time, we decided to get married. We were married 3 ½ years in a very destructible relationship. I was mentally, emotionally, and sexually abused. He lied, cheated, and made me feel as if I were less than nothing and no one would ever want me. Even after we divorced, he still controlled me; and I felt I could never do any better. We brought out the worst in each other. "Hurting people" hurt people, and that's all I knew. I felt that I couldn't trust anyone, and so I hurt people to keep others from hurting me.

Now I found myself a single mom with two little boys depending on me. I worked and supported them, and did everything I knew to love them. I was very protective, and made sure they were always safe. I never got into drugs, but I did drink occasionally; however, I only did this when I was going to be around people. I needed self-confidence, and alcohol provided a crutch. I wouldn't let anyone close to me, and I was very good at using manipulation to get what I wanted when I needed it. This led to doing things that would only make me feel dirty. I thought I was being discreet about it. I played many games and hurt many people in the midst of my messed up life. I was empty and alone with no clue of what real love was. "Love" always came with strings attached and conditions. I always made sure my boys were taken care of, no matter what I had to do. I also worked two jobs to make ends meet. Many men took advantage of me, because I felt I couldn't say no to them. I wanted love so badly!

ENTER GOD'S PLAN!

One day I had been in Ft. Worth shopping with a friend, and I noticed a missed call on my Caller ID when I got home. I called the number back, and a guy answered. I said, "Who's this?" To which he replied, "Well, who's **this**?" Being the hard-hearted woman I was, I said, "You called my phone, so what do you want?" We proceeded to talk, and it turned out that he was looking for my cousin, and was just passing through town. I asked his name, and he said, "Rocky". "Oh yeah," I replied. "That's our new dog's name" that my oldest son had just gotten for Christmas. I felt like he knew that was our dog's name and was joking that it was his name.

Our conversation continued for several hours, and I began to feel something inside I had never felt before in my entire life. He assured me he was a nice guy, but I wouldn't tell him anything personal about me. I was very materialistic and focused on looks. We planned to meet the next day at Red Star Truck Stop. Meanwhile, I contacted my cousin to find out more about this "nice guy". My cousin assured me that he truly was a good guy. I asked if he was good looking because that was important to me in those days. The reply from my cousin was that women flocked to him. I waited all day for him to call, and even had my calls forwarded to my dad's house. (Daddy and my step-mom, Kathy, were going to watch the boys for me so I could meet him.) At last he called, and we met at the truck stop. It was really love at first sight, and we talked for three and a half hours. I never knew real love until I met Rocky. We dated for a year, and were hardly ever apart and never had any fights. His family loved my boys and me. It was really hard for me to receive that love.

I was having some female problems at this time, and was told I needed a hysterectomy or to get pregnant to stop the severe pain. Being the stubborn, selfish person that I was, I decided to have the surgery. Rocky begged me not to have it, he told me we could get married and start a family. His sister, Leigh even called to talk to me about getting a second opinion, but I couldn't hear them. All I could think of was if something happens to me, who's going to take care of my boys?

Our relationship ended, but after a month we started talking again on the phone. He knew the right way to live, and I knew nothing. He had wandered away from his Christian raising, and had lived a worldly life. He had never been married except to his work, and traveled all over with his horses. Although we didn't fight, we were both selfish in our own way. Each of us wanting what the other could not give. In the second summer that we were dating, I was preparing to send my oldest son to my mother's for the summer, and the youngest to his dad's (as this would lessen the financial load on me for a couple of months) when Rocky offered to keep Cameron, the oldest son with him. He said he had a gentle horse that Cam could ride, and he would bring him back during the week and on weekends. I'm not sure why I trusted a man who had never had kids to take mine off like that, but I did. I just had a peace about this guy.

A year went by, and even though we grew closer together than before, we both still had issues from our past, and decided to call it quits. We were separated for three months, and we had gone on with our lives when a chance meeting on the side of the road put us back to talking again. It was hard to pick up where we had left off, so we soon stopped trying. Later as fate would have it, we ran into each other again. Rocky was trying to find my cousin once again, and Cam and I were on a back street going to my grandmother's house when we met him pulling a horse trailer. We began talking again. Little did I know, but he went home that night and prayed. He prayed that if I were indeed the girl for him, that God would have to bring me around because he was finished trying. That night I had an uncontrollable urge to see him. I knew I really loved him, and that it was different than ever before. So the next morning Cam and I drove to where Rocky lived during the week while working in Abilene. We spent the whole day walking and talking about the things that we both wanted to be different in our relationship. He had started attending a church again, and said he wanted to live right. I wasn't sure what that meant, but I was happy to be together again. I also knew I had had enough of the other lifestyle and wanted a change. We began church hopping trying to find one where we felt comfortable. We never did find a permanent place that we attended. Some of the ladies I worked with suggested that Rocky might like the church service they were having at the Sale Barn. The first time he went, he sat in his pickup and listened from outside. The next week he went in and sat down, and that night he rededicated his life to Christ.

A STRANGE TURN OF EVENTS

One day the ladies I worked with invited me to hear a Christian comedian named Chonda Pierce. She came to a near-by town, and I decided to go with them. She was very funny, but then she got serious; and I'll never forget she sang the song, The Potter's Hands. I began to weep and weep, and I **got saved that night! I asked Jesus to be my Lord and Savior, and _my life changed forever_!**

In spite of the fact that I had never known what love was, that night, and still today I feel HIS unconditional love every day. Up until that night, I never cried unless I was mad.

The Holy Spirit started convicting me of my lifestyle, and I wanted things to be different. I started seeking God and reading His Word. I wanted to live a life that pleased Him. The following Valentine's Day, Rocky asked me to marry him!

That was February of 2001, and Rocky and I got married in July that same year. We moved to Abilene, and started our life as a family. When I looked at his family, I thought, "Oh dear, they are perfect like the 'Leave it to Beaver' family." They welcomed my boys, poured unconditional love on all of us, and never judged my past. Their entire family was so loving. Rocky had never been married, so of course, he had no children. I wasn't the model wife for him; divorced with two boys, so they knew I had baggage and a past.

However, God was so faithful, and knew what He was doing. After we married, we rented a house from Rocky's friend "until it sells" as we couldn't afford to buy it, since it was a very expensive house.

After living there a year, the friend called on a Sunday afternoon and said, "We are all brothers and sisters in Christ. My wife and I feel led to sell you the house for what we owe on it." This was such a blessing because it was about one third of the value of the house. We praised Jesus!!! And bought it!

One day as I was on my way home, I was praying and asking God, "What is a testimony? I don't have one." Remember, I never cried, but now I broke and started seeing my life before my eyes from the time I was a baby through all the pain and suffering. He showed me that He was there, walking me through all of it, and I never had a clue! So, I was learning, and He was pouring His unconditional love on me...so overwhelming! I realized that I did have a testimony! I then began having dreams and visions, and didn't understand it all; but I knew He was showing me things, so I would pray and ask, "Now, what do I do with this?"

UNFORGIVENESS / MOTHER

As I was growing closer to the Lord, I started praying for my entire family; but only for the ones I liked. The Lord began teaching me about unforgiveness. I hated my mother and all the others who had abused me. One night, I had a dream about my mother and woke up feeling like I needed to pray for her, yet thought, "Oh no! She doesn't deserve it." I heard the Lord speak to me, and it scared me. It was as if He was behind me, and He said, "If you don't forgive your mother for what she's done to you, then I can't forgive you for what you've done to me." The voice was so intense that I responded, "Lord, I want to forgive her, but I don't know how. Lord, teach me to forgive my mother; teach me how to love her the way you do."

The Bible says in *Matthew 6:14-15*

"If you forgive those who sin against you, your Heavenly Father will forgive you. But if you refuse to forgive others, your Father will not forgive your sins."

So, I started praying for her. It was shallow in the beginning, but God really began to open my eyes to the life she had; how she never had a mother since the time her mother died when she was seven years old. She was passed around from aunt to aunt. I began to truly love her and have compassion for her. This started a healing process in me, and after a year of praying for her, God opened the door for me to talk to her about Jesus. He had been moving in her life already as well, and she was saved! This was totally amazing!

MY DADDY

Since my parents divorced when I was around the age of four, I really didn't know my daddy except in a surface way even though he loved me as much as he knew how to. He had remarried and had another daughter with his new wife. Drinking had become a part of his life even before I was born. This was how I had seen him cope with problems throughout my life.

He started having heart trouble at the age of 40, and lived with this for the last 19 years of his life. He ended up being diagnosed with kidney cancer and bladder cancer the last two years of his life.

The last five years of his life were very special to me because I was able to have the kind of relationship with him that I had always desired. By this time, he was no longer drinking excessively. I helped my step-mom take care of him towards the end, and words can't express what God did! One thing that impressed me is that my daddy was so cheerful through all his sickness and never complained. He loved to laugh and would often make others laugh just because he was laughing.

Two years before Daddy went to be with the Lord, I had a dream of his funeral. It was very detailed, and the Lord showed me He wanted me to speak, which really freaked me out. I was able to share the dream with Daddy, and he was amazed.

We had some amazing talks, and I got to spend very precious quality time with him and really got to know him. I would stay with him at the hospital, and I would go to Eastland to stay overnight with him when he was home while my stepmother was at work. I was very blessed and honored to get to do that. Rocky was very supportive, and he never complained about me being gone so much.

One day I had taken Daddy to Abilene to see my oldest brother who was in prison. Out of the blue

Daddy said, "Will you promise to do something for me?" I said, "Well, of course, Daddy, what is it?" He said, "When I'm up there, will you promise to put cologne on me every day?" I said, "Where?" He looked at me, and I said, "In the funeral home?" He said, "Yes." I said, "Of course I will. Is there a certain kind?" He said, "Yes, I've been saving this Passion for Men, and want this kind. It's my favorite." Wow, for me to be able to keep it together was all The LORD!!! This was in August 2010, and he went to be with Jesus April 16, 2011.

I praise Jesus for allowing me to know that my daddy was saved! Just two weeks before he passed away, he told me that he had felt a presence in his room during the night. He said he thought it was the Lord coming to take him home.

Daddy's funeral was like a huge celebration of his life. He was a very good man, and I give all the glory to the Lord for allowing me to have that precious time with my DADDY! I did share at his funeral, which proved to be one of the hardest things I've ever done in my life. Praise Jesus that I wasn't alone. We all have that appointment. Are we ready to go with no regrets of how we are living our lives? My heart seeks to be more like Jesus everyday. I know I'll never get there until I go to be with Him.

Update

On October 29, 2014, I was asked to speak at First United Methodist Church in Eastland, Texas. When I shared part of my personal story, I mentioned the wreck I was in when I was 16 years old. Afterwards, a man came up to me almost in tears and told me he knew I looked familiar to him when he had met me earlier that night. He told me he was a fireman who worked my wreck that night, and he said he remembered how messed up my face was. We both just stood there with tears in our eyes praising Jesus for the miracles He had worked in my life!

Chapter 2
Jail Ministry

" And whatever you do, whether in word or deed, do it all in the name of the Lord Jesus, giving thanks to God the Father through Him. "
Colossians 3: 17

~~~~~~~~~~~~~~~~~~~~~~

One day at Cowboy Church, shortly after we were married, they announced they would be participating in a jail ministry for the women's jail in Taylor County. The jail had opened up a slot for them to start doing services on Thursday nights on a rotation basis with other churches in Abilene. When the jail ministry was mentioned, something inside me leaped, and I knew I had to do it. Well, I thought WE were called to do it. I quickly learned that Rocky and I have different callings.

I was so scared the first time because I was supposed to speak. But when I got in there, I didn't want to leave! God put a burning desire in my heart to help these ladies. It felt like being at home, and it still feels that way today. I fell in love with the ladies, and my heart broke for them. I started filling in to do Bible studies and church rotation services. I started going and helping on Saturdays, too. I was soon doing some one-on-one mentoring with ladies there. I even started writing to them as they would pull chain to prison just to stay in touch and try to continue to help them. They usually went on to Texas Department of Criminal Justice or Dawson State Jail.

This began my ongoing jail ministry, but it just wasn't enough. The women would get out and go right back to the lives they had lived before. For many, it was a revolving door. There were no Christian based halfway or transitional houses in Abilene. I cried out to the Lord and asked Him, "How can I help these ladies more in order to really make a difference in their lives?" At that moment, I had a vision of a house and a man. I started praying, researching, and seeking God's wisdom on what to do and how to do it. I still continued to go to the jail five days a week. For six years, I prayed and prayed and waited on God's timing. I knew it was going to happen and that it was getting close, but in the physical, it didn't look like anything was happening.

Life Skills Class

When Les Bruce was elected for sheriff, he came to me at one of the Jail Ministry meetings, and asked me to teach a Women's Life Skills class. I was about to tell him only if it was a Christian based deal, and he said, "I know, I know you," and I told him I would check into it and get back with him. I went through training with Prison Fellowship to teach the curriculum, and I have now been doing Life Skills twice a week for five years.

In Life Skills, there are two different groups of ladies, and we usually start with approximately 30 in each class. The jail makes certificates, and we have cake and punch, and watch a Christian movie after they complete a seven-week class. Many of the ladies have never completed anything like this, and it's been very rewarding. After completing the class, some have even had favor with the judge reducing their sentence time.

I have met some very special ladies in Life Skills, and some have come to New Beginnings as well. I really felt like we needed to have this for the men as well as the women, and after praying about whom to ask, I talked to a brother in The Lord, David Jolly. He went through the training, and started the same class for the men. It's so amazing to see all the doors open up to be able to help more people!

Kim – "My Black Daughter"

When I first met Kim, she was in my Bible Study in Taylor County Jail. She had been in gangs, and was in a really bad place. She had also been in drugs for many years. God connected us, and she would get onto the others if they were talking in my class or she would give them "the look".

Kim and I started talking twice a week and ended up getting really close. She got out of Jail a week before Thanksgiving and was planning on going to the Good

News Camp, but they were closed during the holidays due to not having anyone to work. (This was before New Beginnings.) I talked to Rocky and he said it would be fine for her to stay at our house until after Thanksgiving when the camp opened.

I went to County Jail to pick her up. We were so blessed to have her with us. She started calling us Mom and Dad, which honored us since her real mother had passed away and she never had a relationship with her real dad.

She spent Thanksgiving with us along with another one of my special girls, Debbie who we picked up from the restitution center so she could be with us.

Kim went to the Good News Camp for 21 days, and was doing amazing. We stayed in touch until I knew she had fallen, but she wouldn't be honest with me. I told her I was done. Several months later, she called me on Mother's Day crying and asking me to forgive her. She said her life had been hell since she had lied to me.

God truly transformed her life. She has never been the same! She got married to a godly, Christian man, and Rocky walked her down the aisle. Her relationship has been restored with her family, kids and grandkids. We are so humbled at God's amazing grace!

Casey

In 2010, after opening the first New Beginnings house, I met Casey in Taylor County Jail. At this point, she had been in and out of jail several times, so she finally decided to come to New Beginnings. Our house was located just blocks from her old neighborhood, so she didn't last long.

I continued to pray for her, and she would stay in touch with me by calling on occasion. One time she called me when she was really messed up and could barely tell me where she was. When we went to pick her up, we found her in a bar in a very bad situation. We took her to the New Beginnings house, but she wouldn't go inside, so we sat her on the porch.

I left another girl sitting on the porch with Casey while I went inside to change. While changing, I had a vision of Casey running in front of a car, so I hurried back out there to find that she had tried to run in front of a car. But right before she got to the street, she had fallen down. Praise Jesus!

The other girl and I physically fought with her for two blocks and across two lanes of traffic because she wouldn't let me take her anywhere. I was not going to let her die, so I finally told her I was going to call 911 because she would at least be safe in jail. She told me to go ahead as she took off running. Once again, we chased her and tackled her, but this time, we sat on her to hold her down until the cops got there. I felt terrible, but I knew it had to be done in order to save her life.

The next day when I arrived at the jail to do some one-on-one mentoring, Casey came walking up to my car. She had no memory at all of what had happened the night before. She had been in a blackout! I praise Jesus for literally saving her life!

I got Casey in a Discipleship program in Dallas because she felt she needed to be in a different location than her "old life". She stayed there two and a half years, and is now back with me at New Beginnings and is doing amazing. I'm so thankful! She is truly my daughter sent from the Lord!

Chapter 3

Being confident of this, that He who began a good work in you will carry it on to completion until the day of Christ Jesus." Philippians 1: 6 (NIV)

~~~~~~~~~~~~~~~~~~~~~

Rocky and I met Larry and Betty Goff through some mutual friends just shortly after we were married. They were having home church meetings in their house, and Larry came. God connected us in some amazing ways. We started ministering with him late at night in Whataburger fast food restaurants and just wherever The Lord would lead us. After that, he would come to Abilene and stay at our house, and he would spend hours talking to us and explaining God's Word. Rocky and I were both so hungry for Truth. Larry is definitely one of a kind. We really learned so much from him and his wife Betty, too.

Rocky and a good friend of his went with Larry in July of 2003 to the Northwest Territories to minister for two and a half weeks. This was the first time Larry had gone to this area, and they were excited to see the doors God would open for them. They were on a pontoon boat for 11 days, stopping at a wilderness prison camp were the inmates could commercial fish to gain money before they were released. They showed many films, and ate and slept there at the prison camp. Once when they were trying to find a village, they had to enter the Simpson Islands. From above, it must have looked like a rat maze. They were basically lost. They felt they could probably find their way back, but that would defeat the purpose of going. So Larry asked them if they wanted to see what he did in a foreign land. He dropped anchor and got out his fishing pole. He said, "Now, we wait upon the Lord." In just a few minutes, a fishing boat came by. It came from out of nowhere, and it was too windy to pull up beside them. They shouted to them to look for the maple leaves painted on the rocks, and to keep the green ones on the right and the red on their left. When they came back, they were painted on the other side of the rocks – green on right and red on left. They navigated all the way there and back.

I went with Larry to Louisiana after Hurricane Katrina to minister. We stayed in the dome in tents with his granddaughter. We went to see a good friend of Betty's who was diagnosed with cancer. We were able to pray and encourage her as well. It was all so amazing!!! Her cancer went into remission for several years, and then it later come back. She passed away several years later.

Larry felt led to open a camp to help people coming off drugs and alcohol or anyone who just needed help. He opened the Good News Camp on some donated land in a community called Noodle northwest of Abilene. I would go out and help minister to the women. I would also take women out there who had been released from jail so they could get help. One lady I had taken wouldn't eat, so I went out there to spend the night with her. (At that time they had tents and some camper trailers set up, as it was very cold.)

On my way out there, I had a vision of someone coming at me with a big butcher knife. I rebuked the enemy thinking he was trying to attack me with fear. I slept in a very small trailer that night right next to this particular lady. She was up and down all night moving all around, and I slept with one eye open just to make sure. The next day we were all in the pavilion having Bible study when she suddenly got up and ran to the bathroom and then ran out of there very quickly. Larry said, "Grab her!" because he remembered some knives being in that trailer. We ran after her, and we felt she was trying to hurt herself. We finally got her back in, but she was trying to beat her head against the floor. We had to physically hold her down. It took four of us. Another lady was there, but she wasn't helping us at all. She was just praising The Lord with praise songs. I felt that was crazy because we needed help keeping this girl from dying. That was a very scary incident. We ended up taking her to get more help. When one of the other ladies who was still at the camp was cleaning the trailer we had spent the night in, she found a big butcher knife that was under that girl's bed right next to where I had slept. WOW! Did GOD ever protect me!

January 22, 2006, Larry officially ordained me as a Minister. When he called and told me the Lord had put this on his heart, I was very surprised because I had never even thought of it. This really didn't change what I was doing because I was already working with the jail ministry. It did make me official to marry couples and perform funerals, which was way out of my comfort zone.

Chapter 4
God's Touch

"He saved us not because of the righteous things we had done, but because of His mercy. He washed away our sins giving us new birth and life through the Holy Spirit." Titus 3:5

~~~~~~~~~~~~~~~~~~~~

GOD'S HEALING TOUCH

I was working for an attorney in Abilene, and a lady I worked with had a son who was in his twenties who played in a men's flag football league. She was telling me that he had been hit that Saturday, and knocked out. He was taken to the emergency room, and diagnosed with four broken bones in his face. They were sending him to a specialist. As she was telling me the story about her son, it was really impressed on me that I was supposed to lay hands on him and pray for him. I told her, "I really feel led to lay hands on your son and pray for him. Would that be okay?" She said, "Yes, he's a Believer." The next day, which was a Wednesday, he came into the office and I laid hands on him and prayed for him, and I told him that God had healed him. This young man had really strong faith. The Lord actually spoke to me, and told me that because of his faith, he was healed. The next day, he went to his doctor's appointment. When the specialist came out, he asked "Why are you here?" The young man said, "Well, because I have four broken bones in my face." When they took an X-ray, there was not one broken bone in his face! God had completely healed him. This was a beautiful testimony of God's healing touch.

Confirmation

One of the first times I heard God's voice vividly was while I was working for the attorney. It was a good job, but a high-stress job. I had not been asking Rocky if I could quit, but one night he said he wished I didn't have to work, but at that time we couldn't afford for me not to work. The next day at work, I heard the Lord speak to me to put in my two-week notice. I was freaked out because I was thinking about our conversation the previous night.

That night, I told my friend about all of this, and I asked her to pray about it with me. The next morning, I was still in bed when Rocky got out of the shower and said to me, "Do you know what I've heard twice this morning?" I said, "No, what?" He then said, "I feel the Lord told me you are to go ahead and put in your two-week notice." Wow! That was the first time I prayed for God to tell Rocky if it was His will for me, and He did!

CAMERON

One day when Cameron was in the seventh grade and Colby was in fifth grade, they rode the bus home from school. Colby called me at work and said, "Mom, Bub has this girl over that you told him he couldn't see. They are outside smoking cigarettes." We went home, and Rocky and I told Cameron that we knew that girl had been there that afternoon and that they were smoking cigarettes. I didn't tell Cameron that Colby had told me, nor did I say that Colby didn't tell me. I heard Cameron call the girl, and he said, "My mom knows that we were smoking cigarettes." She asked, "How does she know?" He said, "When you have a relationship with God, He talks to you and tells you things. Basically, the Holy Spirit ratted us out." She asked, "What is the Holy Spirit?" It was just amazing to me that Cameron had that revelation, and that was awesome to us! Even though it was Colby who told us, it all came out in the wash!

Another time, Cameron was listening to bad music. He had it hidden in his room, and the Lord showed me where it was. So I got it, and printed out the words, and read them to him. He was very embarrassed after I did that.

ROCKY – "All Things Work Together for Good"

Seasons in life find us doing whatever it takes for our families. The fall of 2004 found us in a season where Rocky was on the road weekly. In 2003, he started an independent business delivering horses for people who would buy them on the Internet. His dad and I would set up pick-ups and deliveries for him. In order to make his trips profitable, we would map out his route all across the United States, so he had several horses to pick up along the way as he delivered others. Our goal was to not let him haul an empty trailer. It was very normal for him to be gone for a week to 10 days at a time. He was on the road so much that one month he only spent one night at home. In the summer, I would ride with him so we could spend time together.

In November 2004, while Rocky was hauling horses, he wanted to take Cameron and me snow skiing for our first time. He had one to drop off and another to pick up in Colorado, so he decided to tie the trip into a family ski trip. We first went to New Mexico, but they didn't have any snow, so we ended up at Wolf Creek Pass, Colorado. We had been skiing all day, and I had fallen all I wanted, so I went in to the little café and waited while Rocky and Cam kept skiing.

While I was sitting there, I had two visions: one was of me driving Rocky's four-wheel drive Dodge Dually down an 8% grade mountain, and the second was that I could see him lying in the snow, hurt. About that time Cam came in and said he couldn't find Rocky anywhere. I told him to go look again. I began praying. Cam came back and said there was still no trace of Rocky. By this time, the café was cram packed with people. I got up to get us a drink, and I saw a paramedic guy walking towards me. Everything went into slow motion, and before any words were spoken, The Lord spoke this to me, *"All things work together for good for those who love the Lord, and are called according to His purpose."* (I didn't know it at that time, but that was Romans 8:28. NL Translation.) A peace fell on me that words cannot describe. I asked what happened to Rocky, and he said, "Well, we have him, and think he has a broken leg." So we headed over to where he was.

When I saw him, he was shivering so badly that his body was coming off the table, and he was totally pale. The most amazing thing was happening though, Rocky, even in this condition, was witnessing to the paramedic guy who rescued him off the mountain, and he had been since the minute he was picked up. A boldness came out of him that I had never seen. We instantly prayed, asking God to heal his broken bones, and for direction. He told me I was going to have to drive him off the mountain because we didn't have insurance, and it would cost $1,000 for an ambulance to take him down to the nearest hospital. I was a nervous wreck! They told me the roads were clear. Well guess what, they weren't!

As we were heading to Pagosa Springs, Rocky told me that the type of pain he was in could cause him to pass out, and asked Cam to lay hands on him and keep praying. As Cam did this, the pain eased up. They couldn't give him anything for pain because I was driving him. When we got to the clinic in Pagosa Springs, they took X-rays, and found that both legs were broken. The right one was shattered from the shin down, and the left had two clean breaks. Rocky was in there asking the doctor if he knew Jesus, and the doctor replied, "Well, I've never had much of a need." Rocky said, "Let me tell you the need." It was amazing to hear him. As they were rolling him out to the truck, Rocky asked the doctor for his hand; and he prayed for the doctor, and he received the prayer.

We went on to Durango where they were waiting for us to do emergency surgery. They took him right in, and Cam and I were in his room waiting for him. Our nurse's name was LUKE, which I found to be very ironic. I started sharing testimonies with him, and I shared the one about when I prayed for a young man whose broken bones were healed. They brought Rocky back in the room after surgery, and he woke up about 3:00am, and he started telling Luke the same testimony I had already shared. Luke said, "I think God is trying to talk to me because I have gotten away from Him for a long time."

They put an external fixator on Rocky's leg and foot to stabilize him. The doctor said it was going be a very long road to recovery. When we asked how long, he said, "If you ever walk again, a year would be pushing it." We told him we didn't receive that because we believed God would work a miracle and heal him way before that. Instantly, we had no income and no savings, and I couldn't work because Rocky couldn't even take care of himself. We cried out to the Lord and asked Him what we were supposed to do. We trusted HIM in every area. We didn't know how we were going to pay our bills, but they were paid on time every time. Sometimes it was right down to the wire, but we would get a check in the mail or someone would come by and say that the Lord put it on their hearts to help us. It was so amazing. I said if we lost everything, we would still trust the Lord, no matter what. Rocky did have another surgery after we were home in Abilene, and they put a metal plate in his right leg. After two months, two weeks and two days, he started walking!!!!! PRAISE JESUS!!!

~~~ *"My God will supply all your needs according to the riches of His glory in Christ Jesus." Philippians 4:19 (NL)* ~~~

After Rocky's accident, we were seeking God's direction for work, for what was he going to do, or what he was even able to do. We received a call from a friend who was working in Arizona, at a Children's Ministry. They needed a manager for the horse program for the kids. Rocky's heart had always been to have a working horse ranch. He told me he felt that God was opening up a children's ministry for him, and we were moving for good. His legs were still weak and swollen. He had a boot on one and a brace on the other one.

Rocky got his proposal together, and then we went to Arizona to meet with the owners. He was still not able to walk a lot at this time as he was still in the healing stages. Rather than take pain pills, Rocky would use crutches when the pain would get to be too much to handle. During the job interview, he left his crutches in the truck so they wouldn't think he was too crippled to work at the equine center. He limped around talking and shaking hands with everyone there, and no one said a word about his legs. It was as if they couldn't see it.

We moved to Arizona. We really believed this was what God wanted us to do, because we had not told anyone we were praying for direction when we got this offer. Still, I heard God in my spirit say something about six months. I didn't understand it, but one day I popped off and said, "Honey, what if we're only supposed to be there for six months?" He said, "Then why pack all this stuff?" I spent days packing things in the house. My closest friend's husband and three sons came to help load the moving truck.

The hardest part about going to Arizona was that Colby, my youngest son, who was only 13 at that time, didn't want to go with us; so he went to live with his dad. That was extremely hard for me to think that he wasn't going to be with us. After all, I'd been with him for all 13 years of his life. Of course, my oldest son moved with us.

When we got there, it was a really hard season because I was away from my son, and I felt like it was a separation. Also, it wasn't exactly what the owners had said. They had told us that they had a job for me, but they didn't. Rocky still wasn't well, and his legs would swell, so I would go out and help him shovel the horse poop in the stalls, or just do whatever was needed. I was glad to do it, in order to help him.

One night while I was asleep, the Lord spoke to me and said, "Get up, and start writing." It's hard to explain. He gave me a message; I had no personal thoughts about what I was writing. I was sitting in the dark so I wouldn't wake Rocky since he had to get up early to work, so I couldn't even see the paper. I didn't have a single thought in my mind, but my hand started writing a message straight from God. He gave me this beautiful message that was a really encouraging word during this dark time in my life.

Here's the word:

May 5, 2005
Missy, Rocky is my servant, and I want his whole heart. I want him to serve me first, and only love you as I love you. You are my chosen ones, beautiful to what I've called you to do. My grace is sufficient for you. I will carry you through even when you don't see me; I'm still there. I'll never leave you nor forsake you. I'm pleased. I LOVE YOU!

After a while, we were still praying for direction, and we felt like our time there was up. We took a vacation to Texas, and went to the river. We were staying at Rocky's mom and dad's house, and just sat down and really prayed and called out to God asking, "What do you want us to do?" No one there knew we were praying for direction. Rocky got a call from this guy who knew Rocky had experience with cattle. He had this deal going, and he offered Rocky a job. We knew this was God, because this guy didn't know we were in Texas, or that we were praying for answers, yet he called Rocky out of the blue.

When we got back to Arizona, we began explaining to the owners that we felt we needed to move back for my youngest son's sake and the jail ministry I had left. They asked us not to leave them without help so they could continue the children's classes and community play days that we had started at the arena. We talked to everyone, but no one wanted it full-time.

Rocky was scheduled to take over the cattle care in November, which would put us in Arizona right at seven months. When he spoke with the guy in Albany, Texas, he was told he needed to contact the cattleman who would be sending the cattle in November. Upon reaching him by phone, he began explaining that his oldest son had left to work clean up in Louisiana from Hurricane Katrina, and he was short-handed. He wanted to know if Rocky could come 30 days earlier and work for him getting cattle ready to go to the wheat pastures.

This nearly created panic in Rocky because he felt honor bound to stay and help the children until someone could take over and continue the programs; after all, God had opened this door first. We were standing in the kitchen just beginning to pray about what to do when the doorbell rang. It was the lady and her husband who had volunteered at every play day we had hosted. Her sister also worked for Rocky at the horse barn. They asked if they could talk to us about taking over the operation. We introduced them to the owners, and it was agreed they would be able to take over so we could move home to Texas October 1st!

When it really got right down to it, guess how long we were in Arizona?   <u>Six months</u>! We had tried to sell our house in Texas, and it just never worked out. Every time we thought it was sold, the deals fell through. Now we understood why it never sold.

It was God's will for us to move back to Abilene. We've been here ever since, and life has just been amazing!

"Do not be anxious about anything, but in every situation, by prayer and petition, with thanksgiving, present your requests to God and the peace of God, which surpasses all understanding, will guard your heart and minds as you live in Christ Jesus." Philippians 4:6,7 (NIV)

Cam's Senior Year

Senior year is the pinnacle of most teenagers' entire high school career. It is typically their last year of living a "care-free" life at home.

Near the beginning of Cam's senior year in high school, Rocky and I knew he had been experimenting with alcohol. We sat him down and explained to him if he was ever drinking and drove, we would take the pickup away and sell it. It was Rocky's pickup he used to drive, and we were making payments and paying the insurance on it, as well as paying for the diesel fuel it used. Rocky specifically told him we did not approve of him drinking, but if he was ever in that situation he should call us and we would go get him. We let him know he would be in less trouble than if he drove while drinking.

This conversation happened on a Thursday. The following Saturday night, a state trooper called me and said he had my son, Cameron. He proceeded to tell me that Cam was drunk, and asked if I would like to go get the pickup before they took him to jail. With my experience working with women in jail, I know that they never call and ask this as they usually impound the vehicles right away. I was very thankful for that, but it was heart wrenching watching him in the back of the state trooper's car knowing he was headed to jail. I was thinking, "That's where I go to minister, not where my son should be." I just couldn't imagine Cam being there.

He called all night wanting us to come get him. We told him we would be there the next day, which was Sunday. We wanted to give him time to think about what he had done, so hopefully, it wouldn't happen again.

Neither one of us could sleep the rest of the night because we were so sick about what had happened to him. We had to call a bondsman and meet him at the jail the next day to bond Cam out. When Cameron came out, he wasn't remorseful at all and had a major attitude. The ride home was incredibly quiet. Rocky said to Cam, "Remember the talk we had on Thursday? That's the way it's going to be." We also took away his cell phone for which we were paying.

When we got home, I started cooking because none of us had eaten anything all day. Cam went to his room, and when I went to check on him, he was packing a bag. I knew he was leaving, so I went to the bathroom and cried and cried and cried. He left on foot headed to the house of a friend who wasn't a good influence at all. It literally ripped my heart into a million pieces. I prayed and released him to God, and prayed He would protect him no matter what.

Cam would call randomly and tell me he was hungry or ask for money. We had agreed that we wouldn't help him with anything as long as he was living like this. Tough love is the hardest thing in the world. He didn't have Thanksgiving with us that year, either. That was the first Thanksgiving we hadn't been together since he was born.

During the day on New Year's Eve, he was weighing heavy on my heart. I told Rocky that I had a bad feeling about Cam. I prayed all day for him. He called out of the blue and told me he was in San Antonio, which made me feel worse. The next day I got a call from my ex-husband saying that Cam had called him, and he had been in a wreck. This was strange because he wasn't even his dad. I finally got in touch with him through his friend's phone and found out they had rolled a vehicle, and it was still under water. God totally protected him once again.

Cam stayed in school, but it was a shaky year. His teacher called me concerned about Cam's grades, so I went to talk to him. We weren't even sure if he was going to graduate in May. It was a miracle, but he ended up making the A/B honor roll.

Right after graduation, he asked us if he could move back home. He told us he was tired of the lifestyle he was living, and he was ready to follow our rules.

Releasing Cam to God was the only way I was able to make it through one of the toughest periods of my life as a parent. Without my faith in God, I don't know how I would have survived this time.

Cameron

As Cam got older, he was sneaking pills and doing different stuff. Rocky had some pain pills left from his accident that he hadn't taken, and it didn't occur to me to think anything of it until one day when The Lord told me to go count the pain pills. I wrote down the numbers of the pills that were in the bottle, and nothing showed up missing for a while. But one day when I checked them, two were missing. I asked Rocky if he had taken them, but he hadn't; he didn't like to take them even when he needed them. I asked Cameron, and he lied to me saying, "No, I haven't taken them." Finally, he did confess, and he told me he took them.

Another time he had been working in Albany, and I had a dream. I dreamed that he died. I even saw what he was wearing in my dream. I saw all the people there; and I saw every detail of his funeral.

Three weeks later, he called me, and told me that he had rolled his truck. I said, "No, you didn't!" Well, he really had rolled his truck, and he didn't have <u>ONE</u> single scratch on him! I read to him the dream I had written after dreaming about his death and funeral. When I read it to him, it freaked him out! I told him that the reason he didn't have a scratch from rolling his truck was God's protection over him.

Another time, Cameron was on Xanax; and he had just gotten married. They had one little girl, and were expecting another. A friend of mine was getting married, and I was going to perform the wedding. It was held in the courtyard at the Grace Museum. It was still a few minutes before time to start the ceremony, and the bride was still getting ready.

A man came up to me and said, "Missy, your boy fell down." I ran from the courtyard through the museum and found Cam outside on the sidewalk. He was having a seizure. They called 911, and as he was having the seizure, I was praying; and I was trying to pick him up. I thought, " If I can just pick him up..." Then he quit breathing. By the time the seizure was over, I think it had been 10 minutes. He wasn't breathing and his coloring was a shade of yellow, and I thought he was dead. A few people who were there for the wedding had come out where we were and some of them physically pulled me away from him. About this time, the ambulance arrived, and I was still thinking my son was dead. I was praying and calling out to the Lord. People started saying, "He's coming back; he's coming back!"

I told Rocky, "You've got to take Cameron to the ER. I just have to do this wedding!" My friend had previously been through so much; I really wanted her wedding to be perfect. Rocky and Cameron's wife, at that time, took him to the ER.

Everyone was still waiting in the courtyard, not knowing what was going on. The bride was running a little late, which was a God-thing. By the time she arrived, everyone had cleared out, and I was just there to say, "Everything is alright!" Every part of me was shaking. I needed to be calm, but I was shaking on the inside. I don't have words to describe how, but I did not do the service; it was the Holy Spirit through me. He did it all. Even though I was a wreck inside, it was amazing how God took over. I also knew that God was involved in bringing Cameron back, in order to give him another chance. He didn't know the Lord at this time. He answered my prayer, and brought him back to give him another chance!

There are so many times that God has watched over Cameron. We have been amazed at God's protection; and how He watches over him. I am happy to say that he knows the Lord now, and has come a very long way. He has two precious little girls. Everything is for God's glory!!!!

I am very humbled, in awe, and just amazed at God's touch, over and over again. He moves in a way we can't comprehend. Our part is to keep going in the way He has shown us to go, to not give up, no matter what; to press in and never give up. Never give up on praying for your children no matter what they are doing or how bad it looks. We have God's promises, and we have to stand on them!

Colby

When we moved to Arizona I knew Colby wasn't going to go with us. He chose to move in with his dad. I had to lay him on the altar, and it was one of the hardest things I've ever had to do. I know the proper seeds have been planted in him. I talked to him daily and came back to visit him a couple of times.

When we finally moved back from Arizona, Colby's father was out of town working a lot, so I started going to stay with him weekly at his dad's house. It was a little over an hour drive from where we lived, but I didn't mind that at all in order to get to spend time with Colby. However, this was very uncomfortable for me not knowing when his dad might come back and just because of our past in general.

Colby never wanted for anything, which made it very hard. Time was the most important thing for him. I was still in his life going to his football and baseball games wherever they were. I would even ride with my ex and his girlfriend at the time when the games were a long way if Rocky couldn't go. Because of the distance, I often had to leave early in the afternoon, and Rocky would still be working. I drove from Abilene to Breckenridge weekly.

In 2011, shortly before he graduated from high school, I found out a girl was pregnant and Colby was one of the guys who could be the father. I talked to the girl, and was able to talk her out of having an abortion, which I found out Colby's dad was going to pay for. I had been through that pain. He and his dad actually got mad at me because of that. I even told the girl that we (Rocky and I) would take the baby if she didn't want him or was not able to raise him. I really felt in my spirit that it was Colby's baby. I did go to one doctor's appointment with her, but per Colby's request, I never went again. That August, she called me when she was in labor, and I went to the hospital. I knew the moment I saw him (Keiton) that he was Colby's. He looked identical to him, and had the same red spot between his eyes, which later went away. This was also quickly confirmed through a DNA paternity test.

I continued to see Keiton, and would even keep him at times. Colby still wasn't happy about it because he wasn't ready for a kid. After all, Colby was only 19 years old. Honestly, during that time, another girl was pregnant and was claiming it was Colby's, too. She would never do a DNA test, so we never felt it was his. There was a lot of confusion for Colby as well, and I believe the enemy tried to get his focus on things that really weren't happening.

Colby's dad didn't really want anything to do with Keiton either, at this point. I finally talked to his dad and told him Keiton was like having Colby all over again. I set it up for Bobby and his girlfriend to go see him. The next thing I knew, Colby was seeing Keiton; and then it wasn't long before he got custody of him. He had been dating a girl who took Keiton in as her own, and they started raising him. Colby has been such a good Daddy.

The hardest part has been that after Colby got custody, he quit letting me see Keiton. He was mad at me, and even though he had Keiton, he wouldn't talk to me at all. I would call, text and send gifts, but got no response.

It has now been three years, and when Colby was about to get married, I tried asking him what I had done to offend him. He sent me a text responding that he didn't like me being there for Keiton's mother, and he felt I spent too much time with the girls in the ministry. I had stopped seeing her but had left the door open for her, as I knew what she was going through; and I had told her we would take the baby. I felt in my heart that he was my grandson and would have done whatever I could to keep him from being aborted. I apologized to Colby, but still nothing changed.

We were invited to his wedding of which I was so thankful. I was able to see Keiton, and it was such a precious time. Colby was like his old self to Rocky and me. I never stopped praying for restoration and healing for our relationship. It's still a work in progress. Thank you Jesus for turning a negative into something so positive.

Chapter 5
New Beginnings

"Therefore if any man be in Christ, he is a new creature: old things are passed away: behold, all things are become new." 2 Corinthians 5:17 (KJV)

~~~~~~~~~~~~~~~~~~~~~~

The Beginning

Four years into praying for the vision God gave me for a women's transitional house, I met a lady who had done transitional housing before, and I shared my heart for this with her. She had previously been in prison, but had now been out for 11 years. Two years later, she moved back to Abilene and told me she wanted to help me with my vision.

We started in March of 2010 with her one bedroom duplex. The very afternoon we decided to do this, my phone rang. A girl left a message on my voicemail that she was getting out of jail and had no where to go. We jumped in the car as soon as I listened to her message, and the Lord led us straight to her as she was walking down the road. A couple of weeks later, we had been out looking at different houses, and the Lord spoke to me twice about one lady named Liz. I had stayed in touch with her after she got out of jail, and she was not doing very well. I heeded the Lord's prompting, and the three of us went to her apartment, not knowing if she even still lived there. Liz opened the door, and said, "I knew you would come." She had been praying for three days asking the Lord to send me, and that's exactly what He did! She had no furniture in her apartment, and told me she was ready to get help. We gathered up her things, and crammed them along with all four of us in my VW Beetle. So now we had three ladies living in a one bedroom duplex. Then Liz's daughter ended up coming, too!

By April, we found a house, and one of the girls felt led of the Lord to pay the $750.00 deposit. Two weeks went by and I had to make a decision by the next morning because I was supposed to sign the papers for this house with this particular lady. The Lord showed me in a dream that night that I shouldn't go forward with her due to a spirit of deception and that her true motive was to make money. I had to tell her the next morning that I couldn't sign the lease with her as a partner. The plan had been that she was going to live there and take care of things first hand. At this point, I was thinking, "Okay, Lord, now what do I do?" He told me to go talk to the homeowner, and He told me I would have favor with him. I was very honest with the homeowner, and I shared my heart with him. I asked him if he would work with me on when the rent was due, and if I could pay it by the end of the month. To my surprise, he said, "Absolutely!"

April of 2010, we moved into the house with three ladies, three blow up mattresses, and a recliner that had been left there by the homeowner. This was the beginning of New Beginnings Transitional Houses ministry. The first house is called Hope House because the women have to have hope to even be able to be there. It's hope for a change.

The minute I took that step of faith, God moved and moved! It was overwhelming watching His provision over and over and over again. I stood in awe of His mighty work because all I had was a willing heart to do whatever He wanted me to do. He is so faithful to make a way when there seems to be no way!

Since that time, God has blessed us exceedingly, abundantly above all we could ever ask for or think of! There were dishes donated from two different people, and they were a matching set! What are the chances of that happening? We experienced so many things like that. I depended totally on the Lord for all finances.

In the beginning, we started with no rules, but that changed very quickly. The women needed structure, responsibility and accountability. I did have them start paying $300.00 a month in rent a month after they started working. When they came from jail/prison, they usually only had the clothes on their backs, so we helped them get everything they needed. When the women came, it would cost about $200.00 each to get them set up with everything they needed, not counting if they needed certain clothing in order to start a new job. In the beginning, we had to utilize help from other resources, but now we are able to do it for them.

I also totally depended on the Lord to show me what was going on in the houses when I wasn't there. My prayer has been that everything that is hidden in darkness will be brought into the light, and it always has been.

One time the Lord woke me up at 11:30pm and told me to go check on one of the girls. I did, and found her drunk. Another time, I popped in at 3:00pm in the afternoon, and both girls were in bed. The Lord spoke to me and told me to look in the trash. When I did, I didn't find anything. Then I heard Him again tell me to look in the trash, so I went outside to look in the big trashcan. When I did, I found beer cans. I woke them up, and told them I knew about it. They were totally freaked out thinking I had security cameras monitoring them or spies watching them. I told them I did, the Lord!

By July that year, I had kicked the last girl out for not following her probation rules. She was sneaking in and out of the windows at night because I didn't allow her to have a key. She was going out of town to see her boyfriend. I nailed the windows shut!

July and August, the house was empty of women, but it was completely full with donations. We held our first annual garage sale that summer. Since there were no women living there, my friends and family and some volunteers helped with it. We sold the things we did not need in order to make money to be able to meet other needs.

By the end of August and first of September, we had more women come to New Beginnings. We had two bedrooms which each had two beds in them. However, most of the time we ended up with six women, so two slept on the couches in the living room. One folded into a bed, but the other was slept on as a regular couch. They would have to make up their couch beds every morning, but they were just thankful to have the couch.

We started having fundraiser garage sales twice a year to raise money to help pay the bills. The girls started getting jobs and helping with the rent. We also began to receive monetary donations, and every month we would have just enough to cover the bills.

This first phase is designed for the ladies to start here with two weeks of down time so they can get adapted to being out and have some time to reflect on why they are there. They also set goals for what they want to change in their lives during this first two weeks. They share a bedroom with another lady at this phase. An important step is to help them attain copies of their ID's, Social Security cards, Birth Certificates and any other documents they need to help them start working on getting a job. We also supply clothes, shoes, hygiene products, make-up, and sometimes medications if they are needed. It is very hard and overwhelming for most of them when they first get out, especially if they have been locked up for quite a while. We take it slow so that it isn't too much too fast. As needs arise, we individualize and help accommodate them to the best of our ability. There are several different places that partner with us by hiring the ladies such as Goodwill, Chicken Express, and Chick-fil-A. Some of the ladies need a longer adjustment period before they are ready to be out in the public and start looking for a job. It is actually a long process since it's hard on most of them now being free, and they don't have a clue how to live.

501c3

I was praying about getting a 501c3 non-profit for my ministry, and found out it was going to cost almost $1,000. One day while we were attending a funeral, my husband began telling a lady about my ministry. She came up to me and asked if I had my 501c3. I told her I had been praying about getting it, and she told me she was supposed to do that for me. The next week I received a check in the mail for $1,000.00 from her. Praise Jesus!

Expansion

The house has a back section that is more like a one-bedroom apartment that the homeowner finally got in livable condition for us after I had three more ladies coming, and I put pressure on him to finish it. I told him that he could finish out the back kitchen later, if he would just get the rest of it livable. By February 2012, we had four ladies living in the front part of the house, and four in the back with one kitchen in between.

That following summer, the kitchen was completed in the back part of the house, and one of our ladies was able to have her son live with her there. They actually lived there for two years before moving out totally on their own.

Phase Two

September 2011, I took the girls on the Walk to Emmaus. One of my girls ended up rooming with a lady who owned two houses that she was renting out to college girls. When she found out about our ministry, she said her houses would be perfect for us. Well, being the stubborn person I can sometimes be, I told her we weren't interested since I had not heard from the Lord that we were supposed to take this step. She mentioned it several times to my girl she was rooming with, but I just kept telling her no.

The following January, she called me and said she had to make a decision, and really wanted the house to be used for good. I thanked her, but again told her I was not interested. We kept talking for a while, and by the end of our conversation, I felt a stirring in my spirit. I told her I would at least pray about her house. To be totally honest, I didn't pray about it because I thought there was no way I could afford an additional $1,500.00 per month in rent plus utilities.

Friday of that week, a local pastor called and said he had a lady who needed help who was broken and wounded, and that I had come to his mind. I told him I would do what I could, but that I had six ladies already and no room to put her anywhere. I finally got help for her through a local women's shelter, but this made me realize my need for more rooms. I then started praying about it, and as I was praying about it, I had a strong feeling I was supposed to open a second house. When I told Rocky about it, he said, "Have you lost your mind?" I said, "Yes, I think I have!" We continued to pray about it, and even went to look at the lady's house. When I saw the house, I knew it was absolutely perfect even though it was a disaster due to the six college girls who were living there. I strongly felt we were supposed to get the house, but honestly, I was a nervous wreck thinking about the extra financial obligation that would come with it. I thought the house was perfect, but it had a swimming pool that seemed a little lavish; after all, I didn't even have a swimming pool! Rocky told me he would support me 100% in whatever direction I felt the Lord was leading me.

Roughly two months later, in March 2012, we had a fundraiser garage sale to raise the deposit money for the house.

Annual Luncheon

In May, we had our first Annual Luncheon fundraiser to raise the money for the first month's rent. We had over 100 people show up at the luncheon, and Sheriff Les Bruce was our guest speaker. The girls shared their personal testimonies with the crowd. All three of the local news stations were there as well as the Abilene Reporter News! We were able to raise the money for the first month's rent! I was totally shocked as once again, God did things over the top!

I was still a nervous wreck about the new financial commitment I was taking on with the second house. One Wednesday night as I was leaving the jail after teaching one of the Life Skills classes, a girl I had only met once waved me over through the glass of her tank. She wanted me to call her out to talk, so I did. She was very apprehensive to talk to me, and I later found out some of the girls had been urging her to share something with me. She wanted me to know that she wasn't very spiritual, and that she had been listening while she was in my Life Skills class that Monday night. She said while she was sitting in my class, she had what she thought would be called a vision. She said she was sitting on a wooden deck around a pool with her feet in the water and one of her children on her left and one on her right. She said there was a wooden fence all the way around, and behind her she saw two double windows. Then she said she saw me walk up. She asked, "What do you think this means?" I immediately began weeping, and told her that was the second house. No one knew **any** details at all about the second house, but she had described it perfectly. After that moment, I had a total peace about the house, finances and all, and I never saw her again.

We were able to move into the six-bedroom, three bath house June 2, 2012. Only the Lord could have orchestrated all the happenings of that day to make our move-in possible. We were blessed with two different groups from Dyess Air Force Base who came and helped clean the house from top to bottom, and they massively cleaned the yard and hauled off trash. They also helped us move things into the house. Many other volunteers showed up to help. It was definitely a team effort getting the house and yard ready and everything moved in!

Mercy House is the name of our second house. It takes a lot of mercy learning to deal with so many other women while working and learning how to live a new life daily. This phase is intended for women to each have their own bedroom (unless we have an overflow and have to bunk up). Everyone in this phase is working and being responsible to pay rent as well as child support if it applies. They are also diligently following all rules of their probation and parole. This is actually top priority in all phases of our ministry. I work closely with probation and parole officers, and have to report if they are not doing what is required. Probation and parole officers also call me from time to time to check up on them. God has given me so much favor with judges as well as probation and parole officers!

Between the two houses, we have the capacity for 16 women, but it's not about the numbers. It's about helping those who truly want a life change. We are prayerful about being able to purchase both houses because this would allow us to help the women more with their transitions into a house or apartment, and with getting their own means of transportation. It's such an honor to be a part of what God is doing in every one of these ladies' lives. I never dreamed He would do such amazing things!

Phase Three

December 2012, I had a dream where I saw two houses. I felt the Lord was telling me through this dream that I was going to have two more transitional houses. I didn't put much weight on this or think about it much because I thought that just couldn't be possible.

In March of 2013, two of the girls came to me, and they told me they felt their "season" was up and it was time for them to move on. However, they said they wished there was a third phase to New Beginnings because they weren't totally sure they were ready to be completely on their own. I began praying about this, and the Lord spoke this scripture to me:

"Don't be afraid, for I am with you. Don't be discouraged, for I am your God. I will strengthen you and help you. I will hold you up with My victorious right hand." Isaiah 41:10

Three weeks later, I saw a "For Rent" sign on a house located very near our second transitional home. I called the number, and left a message. When the lady who owned the house returned my call, I told her who I was and what I was thinking about doing. She immediately got excited, and told me she felt this was a divine appointment of God. She had heard my name in several groups of people, and had wanted to talk to me. She proceeded to tell me about some apartments she owned that she and her husband had shut down in December because the tenants were using them for bad. They had been praying about what they were supposed to do with them. As I was listening to her, I kept thinking that I didn't want apartments; I wanted this house where I saw her sign. However, I started praying about it, and even went to look at the apartments. I then felt God telling me this was our third phase.

I met with the owners one week later to discuss the details, and they offered the apartments for a very affordable rate. The apartments have a total of eight units. We call this phase of the ministry the Freedom Apartments because this living arrangement allows more freedom to live in their own apartment and make godly choices based on the spiritual foundation they have learned from the previous two phases.

We started cleaning up, painting, and replacing carpet on two of the units in May 2013, to get them ready for the two girls to move into. This facility allows them to have their kids for weekend visitations or to move in with them, if they have only one child, so they can be a family once again. They were able to move in by mid June. The girls and volunteers helped me get the third apartment ready by that September. The "We Care Team" at Dyess Air Force Base partnered with us in order to get the next five apartments ready by December that year. They even held a carwash fundraiser to raise money for this project.

This left one apartment that was in the worse shape of all to complete. It was a huge blessing when one of the men who had worked on the Dyess We Care Team volunteered on his own time and used his own money to get this last unit livable. It was completed shortly after the first of 2014.

Phase Three was now complete with eight apartment units for ladies to move into when they were ready for a place of their own, but not quite ready to be totally out from under the New Beginnings umbrella. This is the first time dating is allowed at New Beginnings. I have to meet the guy first, and he is never allowed inside the apartment unless someone else is there with them. This is like they are starting all over and learning a new way of life. If they are married, we require both of them to go to marriage counseling, but he is still not allowed in the apartment without someone else being there. If the husband is not willing to go to counseling, then the wife is not allowed to see him. If they are not married, they are not even allowed to talk to old boyfriends or people from their past who I have not met and approved. It becomes too much of a distraction to them when they are trying to get their lives turned around.

Phase Four

Summer had been with us for close to two years when she was really ready for her two sons, ages 10 and 11 to move in with her. We started praying for a place to accommodate the three of them when we found a very unique house. The front had basically been divided into a duplex with another two-bedroom apartment in the back and a garage. However, the owners wanted much more than we could afford. God had sent a couple to us years before who had been some of our largest financial supporters. They felt led to buy this house in order to help us. We are now renting it from them for a very affordable amount, and it basically pays for itself. These apartments are called Grace Apartments since it takes a lot of grace to function in this phase in order to raise your kids while learning how to be a mom, sometimes for the first time, while working and being responsible for everything.

Knight Carpet donated carpet to us, and Summer's uncle laid it in the two-bedroom apartment. We all, along with some volunteers, worked on painting the inside in order to get it ready for them before school started. Summer and her two sons were able to move in July 4, 2014, which opened up Phase Four. Since then, we have another lady in one of the apartments in the front of the house, and will soon have the other half occupied.

Boots on the Ground Ministry in Abilene is helping get the rest of this house in usable condition. They are converting the garage into a game room for all the kids. They are another big blessing God sent our way!

There are specific rules and requirements with each phase at New Beginnings. We have mandatory Bible Studies and group meetings, but we also love to celebrate together. We have birthday parties to celebrate each other and the new lives they have chosen. Not too long ago, we had a surprise birthday party for Janet's 47th birthday, and after she walked in, she just cried and cried and cried. It was the first birthday party she had ever had! She was so touched that everyone cared that much for her.

I celebrate the one-year anniversary of the ladies coming to New Beginnings by making them a photo book or canvas with special pictures on it. When they have been here for one complete year, it is a milestone in their lives.

Christmas parties are wonderful celebrations not only of Jesus' birth, but also with people in the community blessing these ladies and their children. I have been blown away by all the generosity! There have been gift baskets overflowing with items; and even though they contain different items, the ladies always get one that seems custom packaged just for them!

Accountability

Accountability just happens naturally at New Beginnings. The ladies who have been there longer hold the newer ladies to certain standards. They are also like "acting parents" in their lives. We have a No Tolerance Policy, but they also enforce a "No Negativity" policy within the houses.

Giving Back

The community of Abilene has been so giving towards New Beginnings and the ladies in our ministry. It is important to us that we give something back. I want the ladies to know how important it is to serve without receiving anything monetary or physical in return.

We have volunteered at Mission Thanksgiving, which is a huge charity event for the homeless here in Abilene. Our ladies have spent many hours sorting donations so they can be distributed to people in need.

We have partnered with Lucy's Big Burgers for three years now serving at their annual Thanksgiving Dinner they provide for anyone in the community who is alone or without food or loved ones. The ladies from New Beginnings get to experience helping others who are less fortunate.

Our letter ministry is another way we give back. Each lady at New Beginnings writes letters to correspond with inmates from prisons and jails in Texas. They write letters of encouragement and hope, but more importantly, it helps them remember where they once were. Some of the ladies write to as many as 10 inmates at a time.

2014 Banquet

1st Annual Banquet

1st Annual Banquet

Thelma Gray—Guest Speaker- 2014 Banquet

Missy - 2014 Banquet

Banquet Furniture

Banquet Furniture

Kim - 2014 Banquet

Sheriff Ricky Bishop & Lt. Gonzales at 1st Annual Banquet

Baptism

Lana

DeAnna

Clarissa

Susan K.

Casey

Baptism

Krista

Machelle

Grace

Veronica

Baptism Cake

Birthdays and Celebrations

Anne's Birthday

Summer's Birthday

Vivianna's Birthday

Vivianna's Birthday

Machelle's Celebration

Birthdays and Celebrations

Summer's 1 Year Celebration

Janet's Surprise Party

Jamielou's Celebration

Machelle's 1 Year Celebration

Jamielou's Birthday

Missy, Casey and Rocky
Casey's 1 Year

Birthdays and Celebrations

Jes' Party Group Picture

Betty's Surprise Birthday

Anne's Birthday

Machelle's Birthday

Group Picture

Casey's 1 Year

Children

Missy, Veronica & Son

Machelle with her kids

Jocelyn & son

Stephanie & her daughter

Children

Trish with her kids

Susan with her daughter

Brittany & kids

Grace's kids

Children

Summer's boys

Summer & Tristan

Shana with her daughter

Grace with her kids

Christmas

1st Christmas - 2010

Christmas 2011

Group Christmas 2012

Group Picture 2013

Christmas

Group Picture - Christmas 2013

Missy & Vivianna - Chirstmas 2013

Missy, Anne & Jaimelou

Christmas Party 2013

Group Picture
3rd Annual Luncheon 2014

Fundraisers

Missy & Ma Jo
Art Walk - June 2012

Summer & Casey
Spring 2013 - Garage Sale

MJ & Martha - Spring 2014
Garage Sale

Vivianna, Missy & Jessica
Spring 2011 - Garage Sale

Fundraiser at Lucy's
April 2011

Grandma Lillie & Missy
Garage Sale - Spring 2013

Fundraisers

Stephanie - Garage Sale - May 2014

Garage Sale - Spring 2011

Garage Sale - Spring 2013

Garage Sale - Fall 2013

Fundraiser Sign

May 2014 Garage Sale
Missy & Brittany

Girls with Missy

Susan K., Missy & Clarissa

Anne, Jaimelou, Missy & Reece
3rd Annual Luncheon

Summer, Missy & Casey

Shanna - Court Hearing

Rocky & Kim (Daughter)
Walking Kim down the aisle

Girls with Missy

Missy & Betty

Kim & Missy
at Kim's Wedding

Missy & Kim - November 2014
3rd Annual Luncheon

Brittany, Missy & Trish
Newsboys Concert
October 2014

Girls with Missy

Missy speaking in Colorado City

Praying at house

Missy & Linda
3rd Annual Luncheon

Stop the violence booth

Liz & Missy - December 2013

Missy & Cindy cooking

Group Charity & Events

Becky, volunteer
with Girls - Love & Care

Machelle, Missy & Sara -July 2014
Love & Care - Palm House

Group at Conference
Newsboys Concert
Fall 2014

Craft Night

Miss Martha, Volunteer
Newsboys Concert
Fall 2014

Group Picture
Spring 2014

Group Charity & Events

Glamour Shot - November 2012

Girls at Beltway Pink Impact
May 2011

Group at Conference - Fall 2012

Craft Night

Coloring Eggs - Easter 2012

Luncheons

1st Annual Luncheon

1st Luncheon with Les Bruce
(He was Sherriff then)

1st Annual Luncheon
Veronica

1st Annual Luncheon
All the news came, it was amazing!

Les Bruce
Guest Speaker
1st Annual Luncheon

Susan K.

Luncheons

2nd Annual Luncheon 2013

Summer
2nd Annual Luncheon 2013

Waylan Jackson
Guest Speaker
2nd Annual Luncheon 2013

Clarissa
2nd Annual Luncheon 2013

Vivianna
2nd Annual Luncheon 2013

Luncheons

Missy
3rd Annual Luncheon 2014

3rd Annual 2014 Luncheon

Linda
3rd Annual Luncheon 2014

Summer
3rd Annual Luncheon 2014

Luncheons

Anne
3rd Annual Luncheon 2014

Reece
3rd Annual Luncheon 2014

Jamielou
3rd Annual Luncheon 2014

Missy's Family

Rocky, Keiton (Grandson), Missy & Colby (Son)

Rocky, Keiton (Grandson) & Missy

Rocky, Missy, Lainee & Bayleigh (Grand daughters)

Missy & Colby (Son)

Missy & Her Daddy

Missy's Family

Missy & her Mother

Missy in wheelchair

Cam, Kourtnie, Lainee & Bayleigh

Cam & Missy

New Beginnings Houses

#1 Hope House

#2 Mercy House

Dedicating Mercy House

3 Freedom Appartments

#4 Grace Apartments

New Cars

Susan's New Car

Summer's New Car

Casey's First Car

Veronica's New Car

Summer's Smile

Summer & Dr. Hawley

Summer's Smile

Veronica's Smile

Veronica & Missy

Dr. Hawley, Missy & Veronica - Smile

Thanksgiving

Lucy's 1st Annual

Rocky & Missy
Lucy's 2012

Serving at Lucy's
Thanksgiving 2012

2nd Annual Lucy's
Thanksgiving 2013

Jamielou & Missy
Lucy's - November 2014

Leslie & Missy Lucy's 2014

Thanksgiving

Lucy's 2014 Group Table

Lucy's- November 2014

Stacy & Missy
Lucy's - November 2014

Rocky & I Thanksgiving 2014

3rd Annual Lucy's Thanksgiving

Thanksgiving

Lucy's 3rd - November 2014

Lucy's 3nd - November 2014

Summer & Missy
Lucy's - November 2014

Lucy's November 2014

Volunteers

Volunteer - Brandy

Buffi at Luncheon

Missy & Miss Wanda

Marilyn

Janet & Terry

Becky

WTU / KTXS
Volunteer Citizen of the Year

TV

WTU - Check

WTU

WTU

Craft Night

Chonda Pierce

Missy & Chonda Pierce

This was so amazing! I was able to actually meet Chonda Pierce at Gateway church. 15 years after I got saved at one of her concerts.

Pulling Chain

Leigh & Missy

This was after all the editing "Leigh was able to pull chain".
She learned a whole new language during her time
working on the book.

Chapter 6

Devine Interventions

" For I know the plans I have for you,' declares the Lord, 'plans to prosper you and not to harm you, plans to give you hope and a future.' "
Jeremiah 29:11 (NIV)

~~~~~~~~~~~~~~~~~~~~

Lady in the Road

Late one night, as I was on my way home from teaching the Life Skills class at the jail, I vaguely saw something out of my peripheral vision on the left side of the road. All of a sudden, I realized it was a woman as she darted out in front of my car! She was so close, I could have touched her! Needless to say, my car almost hit her. When I turned around and went back, she had fallen in the middle of the road. I got out and tried to get her to the side of the road. She was wasted drunk and had cactus all in her. A man who lived close by stopped and helped me get her to safety. He said he had suddenly felt a strong urge to go workout, which was much later than normal for him. I told him that God knew I needed help and had sent him. We called and got help for her. She was extremely mad at me and told me that I ruined it for her because she wanted to die that night. I said, "NOT on my watch! God sent me to help you, and you will live and not die." I never saw her again.

Suicide

One time a lady who had been in and out of jail several times called me in the middle of the night. She was contemplating suicide, and I was able to talk and pray her through until someone got to her. I honestly had forgotten about this until she ended up back in jail several years later to sit out some tickets, and she shared about that time and told how God so powerfully intervened that night.

Be Led

One time when I was with a friend and we were praying for some people, she wanted me to go and pray for this particular guy. I honestly did not feel led to pray for him.

I felt obligated to go because my friend really wanted me to go, so I went anyway. While we laid hands on him, I had my eyes closed; and The Lord spoke to me and said, "Open your eyes!" When I opened them, he was about to touch me in an inappropriate area. I said, "Don't you dare!" I learned a valuable lesson that day. Be led by The Lord in ALL things, not by people!

Century Lodge Hotel

I was out ministering with a friend about midnight one night at the Century Lodge Hotel. We were ministering to a couple who were staying there. We had gone to get food for them, and had just gotten back and were talking with them when all of a sudden; we heard a lot of commotion outside. I could hear the police kicking in doors and busting people who had drugs. They were arresting people right there at the hotel. I felt sick at my stomach. I had been to the jail that day to do a Bible study, and I had been to visit my brother at the prison in Abilene. All that kept going through my mind was that I was going to be taken to jail because I knew this couple had drugs in there. I immediately started praying. When the police got to our door, they knocked which shocked me. The lady said for them to come in, so in walked two police officers. I immediately told them who I was and what we were doing there. They asked the people if they had any drugs in there, and the lady quickly said, "No, sir. No, sir." I knew she was lying, but the officers said, "Y'all have a good night. Sorry to bother you." Whew!! That was close! That really scared me. I asked them if they realized we all could be on our way to jail. Her husband went to the bathroom and flushed whatever they had.

Century Lodge Hotel – 2

Larry Goff and I took some teen-agers out to minister one night around 2:00am. We drove around the Century Lodge Hotel, which was unusually quiet for this time of night. When we pulled around to the other side, we could see a girl. Larry stopped, rolled down his window, and asked if we could pray for her. She said sure. He had barely gotten started when we heard a girl screaming. The girl we were praying for said, "That's my sister in a fight with my boyfriend." We backed up and got out of the car. I looked at the girl and recognized her from jail. I called her name, and she answered me. I got a blanket to cover her because she was not clothed. I sat on the bed with her trying to calm her down while Larry was talking to the guy. She got mad all over again, and started trying to fight him again. I physically grabbed her and held her so she couldn't move. Larry and the guy went outside, and I helped her get dressed so we could take her somewhere else.

The young kids who were with us never got out of the car because they were so freaked out.

As we were walking outside, I saw a truck pull in with a lady I knew. By this time it was about 3:00am. I went over to the window and tapped on it. She freaked out. I asked her what she was doing she said, "I'm up to no good!" Later she told me she had just gotten high, and I had completely ruined it. Woo Hoo, thank you Jesus!!!

Birthday Blessing

February 19, 2010

My "Birthday Blessing" is that I am still here! I was on my way to Rocky's office to answer the phones for him today, and just as I exited off one road before I could turn to get up on the freeway, my car died for no apparent reason. It didn't sputter or act strange at all, it just died. I had just barely gotten out of the road and tried to restart it twice when all of a sudden, a white Chevrolet pickup came flying through the red light. He was going so fast that when he hit a dip in the road, it sent him airborne! When he landed, he was still going and uprooted two trees before he finally came to a stop. This all happened just 20 feet in front of my car! If my car had not died when it did, I would have been in the exact spot for him to hit me when he was airborne! I sat there in total shock! I didn't even call 911. I finally called Rocky, and as we were talking, a friend of Rocky's passed by and called Rocky. He then turned around and picked me up.

God's protection is so real that we often don't even realize the danger that could be ahead! I know there are times He protects us when we never even know it or see why something happens such as my car dying when it did. When my car was checked, there was nothing wrong with it at all. Rocky and a friend of his did put more diesel fuel in it, even though it wasn't out, and they finally got it started.

Wedding Ring

Not long after Rocky and I got married, he started selling insurance with Aflac. We went with some friends to Huntsville to the trustee camp for open enrollment for them to sell insurance. The other wife and I had been walking all around outside where there were millions of small rocks. When we went back inside, I looked down and the center diamond was out of my wedding ring. My heart sank because all I could think about was how much it had cost and how special it was to me.

I immediately started praying for God to show me where it was. We started back outside, and the guard said, "You look like you lost your puppy dog." I said, "It's worse. I lost the set out of my ring, but I'm going to find it." He laughed and said, "Good luck with that." Well, we went back outside and walked all around talking and praying. We finally stopped and when I looked down, the diamond was right in front of my shoe! It looked very small in the midst of all the rocks and gravel. The guard couldn't believe it when I went back in and showed him that I had found it! He was shocked! I said, "**That** is answered prayer!"

God even cares about the "little" things in our lives that matter to us, but seem so small compared to Him!

Jeep Tire

One day I was driving to take my youngest son, Colby to a place near Abilene where his dad kept some horses, so Colby could feed and water them. We both kept hearing a knocking noise on my Jeep the entire way there. Several times, I stopped and we got out to try to find what was making the noise, but we never could find anything wrong. While I was sitting there waiting for Colby to water and feed the horses, I had a vision of my tire coming off. Since I wasn't sure what that was supposed to mean, I prayed for protection over us all the way home.

Rocky had been out riding his Harley when he felt impressed by The Lord to come home and check the Jeep because I had told him what was going on earlier. After checking the Jeep, he came into the bedroom in tears and grabbed my hand. All of the lug nuts had come off of my wheel except for one, and it was hanging on by the last thread.

Talk about PROTECTION!! It was a ragtop Jeep, so it could have been really bad!

Praying for Timmy

I had been praying for Timmy, my oldest brother, and would have many dreams about him and what he was doing. This totally freaked him out when I shared them with him. I would have to drive to Eastland on many occasions just to tell him the dreams, again.

One night, while staying with my daddy, I stayed up most of the night talking to Timmy trying to help him change his life and trying to get him to stop doing drugs and all the other stuff he was involved with. About 6:00am the next morning, I woke up and had a strong urge to pray for him. I did and then went back to sleep. He called my daddy around 7:30am that morning panicking and wanting to talk to me before I went home. When I finally got up, I went by to see him on my way home. He asked me, "Have you been praying for me?" I told him I always pray for him. He said, "No, I mean this morning." I said, "Yes, as a matter of fact I did pray for you this morning." He then said, "I've been cussing you all morning because I've been trying to shoot up, and I can't get the needle to go in!" He showed me his arms and legs, and I said, "PRAISE JESUS!" We talked for a while, and he cried and told me he wanted to stop, but he didn't at that time.

The night He was caught

The night Timmy finally got caught, I had a dream I was in a big building with him and I was begging him, "Please don't steal; please don't steal." I woke up from my dream in the middle of the night, and I prayed the rest of the night for him because I knew whatever it was, it was bad. The next day he called and said they had picked him up. Later, he thanked me for praying for him. That same night, they were planning to steal from the Mexican mafia, but he was caught before they could go. He said he could have run to escape being caught, but he fell to his knees. I know God protected him because odds are if he had gone through with his plans, he would have been killed that night. Even though it was prison, God saved his life that night.

He later got PUSH tattooed on his arm, which means 'Pray Until Something Happens'.

All glory goes to Jesus!!!

May 2013 Car Break-in

I had a dream I was driving Rocky's old 1972 Chevy pickup truck. In the dream, I had left my purse in the seat, and someone came and tried to grab it while I was talking to someone else, but I caught them. I turned back around, and then they tried to get my wallet.

The next day I was thinking the entire day about how I needed to be extremely cautious, as that dream had probably been a warning. I was exceptionally careful all day. That evening, I went to the jail to teach my Life Skills class. I had gotten in a hurry and left my Prada purse on the seat instead of hiding it out of sight. (We aren't allowed to take anything inside except our ID and books for class.) When I came out, it was still daylight and someone had busted my passenger window and took my purse. I felt sick because a dear friend had given me that purse. (I didn't even know what Prada was until one of the ladies saw it and told me that it was an expensive brand purse.) Thank goodness my phone and makeup bag were not in it at the time. I did have a large deposit for New Beginnings along with my wallet full of cards and checks and even more cash. They do not have cameras outside the jail, so there was no way to know anything specific that had happened at that time. For a woman, trying to recall everything in your purse is extremely hard and so very personal! I also had my spare car key in there. I instantly felt like God had warned me, and I had let Him down. I was in a real battle. I did instantly start praying for all who were involved, and that God would use this for good. This is not easy to pray when you feel so violated.

Three days later, a girl in jail, whom I had known previously, put in a request to talk to me. I also knew that when she was arrested, she was caught with one of my old ID's and my Social Security card. She started telling me all her problems and that she needed somewhere to go and on and on. I said to her, "Do you realize that I know you got arrested with my things?" She replied, "Yes", and she never even blinked an eye. It was as if it didn't register with her. I said, "Well, the first thing I require at New Beginnings is honesty, and I don't think you're there yet."

I continued to watch her really change and grow while in jail. It was a huge headache handling everything. They had written checks on the New Beginnings account all over town, and it was a real pain to go through straightening everything out. I also still felt so violated.

One day, I was walking into a store not praying or anything when I heard The Lord tell me that it wasn't a warning, but He was preparing me. WOW! That changed everything! I felt His love and compassion for the people who were involved. By this time, I knew everyone who was involved with the girl. There were five people, and they had written over $10,000 worth of checks.

What satan meant for harm, God will turn for His good for His glory!

The girl started writing me after going to prison, and asked if I would help her. She was going to have to serve about a year in time. I had a compassion for her and told her I would. We couldn't let any of the others know because they would not be so nice to her since they are very protective of me. So we kept it hush-hush.

She told me they bonded her out of jail with the $1,100.00 cash, but she ended up going right back two days later.

When she came to New Beginnings, she had gotten some of her things from where she was staying and some of my stuff was still there, but nothing major. I still didn't get the purse back or my wallet or any of my other valuables. What a blessing that God can turn every situation into good if we will be willing to forgive and walk in His love and compassion. No, it's never easy, but lives can be changed and transformed in the midst.

Chapter 7
Three Years of Pain

"For He Himself has said, 'I will never leave you nor forsake you.'" Hebrews 13:5b (NKJV)

~~~~~~~~~~~~~~~~~~~~

My three years of pain all started in May of 2011, just a few short weeks after my father's funeral. I joined a boot camp with my friend thinking I would get in shape and start eating healthy. Well, that's not at all what happened!

The class was twice a week on Tuesdays and Thursdays. On the third day of class, which was on a Tuesday, while working out, I suddenly felt excruciating pain in both feet. The trainer told me just to modify the workout, but I couldn't do it at all. I ended up sitting down for the remainder of that class. By Thursday of that week, I finally went to a walk-in medical clinic. They gave me Prednisone, which I later learned the dosage was way too much. Saturday, two days later, I went to the Emergency Room to no avail. The clinic called me back and said that my blood work wasn't normal and that I needed to see a doctor. This presented a big problem getting in with a doctor since I didn't have insurance at that time.

I was in so much pain and barely walking when two weeks later a lady brought a wheelchair to me. As much as I didn't want to be in a wheelchair, it was a blessing because I was in too much pain to even stand, much less walk.

Words cannot describe what I really went through. The battle was on! When it first happened, the Lord said to me, "My grace is sufficient for you in your time of need."

"But he said to me, 'My grace is sufficient for you, for my power is made perfect in weakness.' Therefore I will boast all the more gladly about my weaknesses, so that Christ's power may rest on me. That is why, for Christ's sake, I delight in weaknesses, in insults, in hardships, in persecutions, in difficulties. For when I am weak, then I am strong." 2 Corinthians 12:9-10 (NIV)

I stood on this scripture every time the enemy put thoughts of suicide in my head. I would be attacked with these thoughts of driving off the bridge many times when driving home or swerving into oncoming traffic. I would also be attacked with thoughts of just giving up New Beginnings and letting it go, or of stopping my jail ministry. I fought depression and feelings of being unworthy.

I would praise Jesus and remind Him of what He spoke to me! People would come and pray for me, but I would feel worse. They would tell me that I just needed to have "faith" and "to believe and stand on God's Word." They had no idea how much faith it took to just take one step with the pain I felt. I couldn't listen to some "religious" people who thought they were being encouraging. I'm not talking about Spirit filled Believers, I'm talking about people who act all religious and don't understand what real faith is because of rules and regulations, not true freedom in Christ. They made me feel condemned like I had done something wrong. Jesus never came to condemn for any reason.

"So now there is no condemnation for those who belong to Christ Jesus. And because you belong to Him, the power of the life-giving Spirit has freed you from the power of sin that leads to death." Romans 8:1-2

When all else fails, we must keep standing on Him and His Word only. As I was in the wheelchair, I would see people stare and talk about me. It's not like having a broken leg or something evident that you can see what is wrong. People don't understand pain unless they can see something broken. I guess that was one of the hardest things to endure because a lot of people did not understand at all what I was going through. It hurt to stand, walk or sit. The best I would feel was when I was flat on my back. I even started losing my hair, which was scary as well. I told God, "No matter what, I'm still going to serve You, in pain and with no hair. Nothing will stop me from doing what

You have called me to do." I never stopped believing that I would be healed. I believe in super natural healing, and I also believe God uses doctors to heal.

During this time as well, Rocky stood by me and was so full of patience because I wasn't always the best person to be around. His mother, Jo took care of me during that time, too. She was such a huge blessing. When it first started, I would go over to her house during the day, and go home when Rocky got home from work. Not long into this, our air conditioner quit working, so we ended up staying at his parents' house for over a month. What a blessing to have someone love and take care of me like Jo did. I wasn't used to that at all as I've always had to be the caregiver. I learned so many things during that time. The most important thing I learned was that God's promise of never leaving us nor forsaking us is real! Going places in a wheelchair and having to ask for help was very humbling.

I kept trusting God's timing and kept doing what He called me to do, even in a wheelchair. I continued going to the jail twice a week to teach my Life Skills class. Jo would drive me to the jail, and the guards would roll me with all my books to class. Either Rocky or my son, Cam would pick me up afterwards. I was even able to do baptisms while in the wheelchair using a horse trough in the jail. What a special time! I would also go over to check on the ladies at New Beginnings, and they would help carry me up the stairs to get me in the house. The love that everyone poured out to me was amazing! Satan comes to kill, steal and destroy, and of course he would love to do that to anyone who is doing God's work. I'm just stubborn enough to keep going and not let anything stop me from doing what God has called me to do.

Over the course of several months, I saw a Family Physician as well as an Internal Medical Specialist, and I still did not get relief from the pain. The doctors came to the conclusion that it was Fibromyalgia because they couldn't find anything else.

Rocky finally took me to Dallas to his sister's doctor who specializes in allergy eliminations and other natural treatments around the first of July. I went back to her near the end of July for a second treatment, and afterwards, she had her husband who is a chiropractor adjust me. After that, I got up and walked out of their office, and never got back in the wheelchair. It was amazing. The severe pain was gone, but this only lasted for a short time. It was much later that I would come to understand why.

The next two and a half years, I ended up still experiencing pain, which lead me to see Massage Therapists, Physical Therapists, other Chiropractors who were located here locally in Abilene, as well as other doctors. It seemed like I was going to have to live with pain for the rest of my life because no one seemed to be able to find the true root of it. Some days, I had to lie flat on my back to get relief. Doctors would give me pain medication that would make me sick and not even begin to eliminate the pain. I was afraid to take much medication for pain because of my mother's addiction to pain pills after her back surgery.

I finally found a doctor who set up two MRI's, one on my neck and one on my lower back. After the results came back clear, they told me it was nerve damage. I figured it was hopeless because most neurologists will not see patients without insurance.

It was January 2014, before I went to a neurologist who noticed a bulging disc. This disc was pressing against my spinal cord causing severe pain all throughout my body. It was a relief after almost three years to finally know what was causing all my pain. However, the treatments this doctor tried made me worse.

In February of 2014, I met a lady who wanted to volunteer at New Beginnings. After showing her one of the houses, we were talking and I mentioned that I was scheduled for injections on the bulging disc in my neck on Monday, just three days away. She told me she worked with a doctor who is awesome and affordable. She talked me into waiting on the injections and seeing this doctor instead. Through lots of perseverance and being persistent with the insurance company, I had surgery on May 12, 2014. Thank You, Jesus for no more pain!

Relief was felt instantly. Now I have a compassion that I didn't have before for people with severe chronic pain. God is so faithful to always make a way when there seems to be no way!

Chapter 8

Blessings Received

"And God is able to bless you abundantly, so that in all things, at all times, having all that you need, you will abound in every good work."
2 Corinthians 9:8 (NIV)

~~~~~~~~~~~~~~~~~~~~

2013 Abilene Volunteer Citizen of The Year Award

Missy Denard does not just give her time to the women in New Beginnings, she gives everything! She is one of the most selfless, loving and compassionate people I've ever met. So, when WTU Energy announced in the summer of 2013, they were hosting a contest for someone in Abilene who was making an impact in their community by volunteering their time, it was no surprise that three ladies from New Beginnings nominated Missy Denard, unbeknownst to her. After multiple interviews with New Beginnings ladies and Missy, it was also no surprise Missy was one of the top five finalists. A local TV station even filmed her teaching a Life Skills Class in the women's jail as well as leading a Bible Study with the women at one of the New Beginnings' houses. She mentors women who are both in jail and after they get out, if they become a part of New Beginnings. Without someone to believe in them, most of these women feel like they will be a product of their upbringing

101

forever. They don't have hope of ever having a better way of life.

Missy was surprised with the news that she won the 2013 Abilene Volunteer Citizen of the Year award on live television through their partner for the Abilene program, KTXS. Her husband, Rocky was able to get her to the TV station for the surprise announcement under the pretense that they needed to do a follow up interview with her. A handful of the ladies from New Beginnings were also there to celebrate with her. They could hardly contain the enthusiasm they felt. It was exciting to see these women wanting to do something to see Missy blessed in return for everything she has done for them. As the recipient of the 2013 Abilene Volunteer Citizen of the Year award, Missy received a $5,000 donation to New Beginnings Ministry, which was another huge blessing!

--Leigh Denard Little

Veronica's Smile

There is a saying that a smile is worth a thousand words. If this is the case, Veronica was silent for six years. She lost her self-confidence along with her smile when her teeth were damaged from a very abusive relationship. However, there are not enough words to describe how she felt when Dr. Hawley who is a volunteer with Texas Dental Association of Smiles Foundation restored her smile through Texas Mission of Mercy Charity at the Abilene Civic Center October of 2013. Their primary goal is to get people out of pain and to prevent pain, but they also restore teeth so people can chew their food, smile, meet the public and get a job.

Upon getting her new teeth, Veronica could not stop smiling, and said, "I can finally eat again, chew my food, have my confidence back. Mainly have confidence. I have a 14-year-old son who's going to be ecstatic that I'm not covering my mouth anymore."

Veronica, who once would not smile for anything, now will not stop smiling. Dr. Hawley blessed her with much more than just a smile. She feels she got her life back!

Summer's Smile

Summer is a beautiful lady, but she wasn't able to see her true outward beauty because she didn't have the confidence to smile. Through many circumstances in her life, Summer's teeth were in such bad shape that she was in severe pain all the time. She went to the charity event hosted by Texas Mission of Mercy in October of 2013, and had all her top teeth removed. Dr. Hawley agreed to work with her on getting top dentures, but because she had worked so hard at improving her life since coming to New Beginnings almost two years earlier, he blessed her with a new smile totally free of charge!

Susan's Car

In June 2014, Abilene had a big storm that produced softball sized hail, which totally destroyed Susan's car. We kept praying about her situation, and felt a peace that God was in control. Susan was in school and didn't have extra income to spend on a new car. The Lord put it on one of our volunteer's hearts to donate a large amount of money which was used to replace Susan's car with another one and also used to repair the windshield to Summer's car that was totally shattered in the storm.

Christmas Baskets

In 2013, I spoke at a women's group at Brookhollow Christian Church. Afterwards, a lady who was interested in hearing more about New Beginnings approached me. We met at a later date, and she told me she wanted to coordinate baskets for gifts for our women in New Beginnings houses. I told her that it would be fine for them to do that, but I really didn't expect to ever hear anything more about it. She called me several months later to tell me she had baskets ready for the ladies for Christmas. I was blown away at how nice the baskets and gifts were when she delivered them. The greatest part was that each basket was unique and was a perfect fit for each of our ladies. I know they thought I had told the lady what to do for each of them, but it was all the Lord.

Craft Night

Monthly craft nights are a huge blessing to all of us at New Beginnings. Brandy meets the ladies at the Mercy House once a month with a variety of craft projects making anything from tile coasters to decoupage crosses to candy jars to re-finishing furniture that we auction off at our annual Banquet. Brandy is awesome with the women teaching them everything they need to know even if they haven't had any experience with crafts before.

Chapter 9
Testimonies of Healing and Hope

"But you are not like that, for you are a chosen people. You are royal priests, a holy nation, God's very own possession. As a result, you can show others the goodness of God, for He called you out of the darkness into His wonderful light." 1 Peter 2:9

~~~~~~~~~~~~~~~~~~~~

Anne

No one would ever nominate me for woman, mother, daughter, sister or friend of the year. Those titles I never earned. I've been far from that mark. I've been a lot of things: I've been a junkie, an abuser, a user, a liar, a cheat, a hooker, a bag hoe, and a dealer...

That is I **have** been.

The things I did when I was lost almost seem like a nightmare that I watched through another's eyes. The pain I once lived seems almost surreal to me now. The little girl being molested and made to do things that little girls should never have to do with men and women… not real. The fear and fright that a brother and sister had to endure while waiting for their turn as they heard the other crying out in pain … not real. The pains of those moments … not real. Days turn into years… the past of foster homes, family being murdered, older brothers being taken and never

109

seen again... all this, not real. Wondering, watching, who was that who lived in me?

At age eleven, I was already smoking PCP and in a gang trying to find acceptance. And then, being used by yet another man, and another... growing up on the streets... violent. First time I ever seriously hurt someone and I broke his chest plate. I never saw my Ken again. Guilt haunts me. My granny was murdered, and the man who killed her I once loved and called grandpa.

Anger, so much rage... I'm older, I'm stronger, so no one will tell me how to live. Thirteen years old, and I'm already following a path of criminality. I am being sent to RPCC for attempted manslaughter.

Now I'm fourteen, and my mom, who doesn't know how to handle me, kicks me out and I begin to learn prostitution. I stick a needle in my arm. I'm alone. I don't care. I survive. I live and I learn even quicker. I know how to make money... blood sweat and tears.

Twenty-one and on the run, and I've just been busted for a huge dope case which was the second largest in Reno that year. I'm pregnant; I'm dark and bitter. I'm strung out. My baby's life is already marred. I'm too selfish to care. I give birth, and one of the few right things I try and do for her in order to keep her, is turn myself in so I won't lose parental rights; and I do four years.

I'm released, my child looks familiar but we are

strangers. We stare at one another from across the room. That is the basis of how we are our whole lives.

I haven't learned anything, I'm strung out, and dealing dope within a matter of months. I abandoned my mother and daughter. They needed me, but this was not the first or the last time I broke their hearts. This would be a cycle, the cycle of me.

In prison, the women in here knew more of me than my own family. This second time didn't help anymore than the first. I'm released; my mother has hopes that I've changed. She loves me. My daughter needs me, and wants her mother. Her dad had never acknowledged her. I try, but my cycle happens again.

I'm in prison. This time it's harder. I spend 60% of my time in segregation. I get in so many fights. My institutional points are higher than even murderers on the yard. I almost blinded the last woman who hit me by trying to gouge her eyes out. I'm released. My mom and daughter again have faith in me. My daughter is in foster care, I get her back and I try. I really did.

Some very bad things happened to me and to my family. Some are my fault, some not. I lose my daughter, and everything is taken from me. My family, my home, my animals, everything I love is taken. Even my truck is stolen. I can't grip, so I go back to using drugs. I have a mental break down.

The cycle of prostituting and being with lovers who

were violent continues. Dealing with people who had tried to harm me if not kill me. Armed robbery, forged instruments, dope houses, counterfeit money, running guns and trying to harm if not kill those who stood in my way all is a way of life. All the years I was out there, my family witnessed all of it, especially my daughter. She has seen me harm a lot of people. She is scared of me. My mother is scared of me. A lot of people are.

I become strung out again. I stay high for years, and end up truly on the streets. Homeless... I have so many lovers I've lost count.

The whirlwind of chaos follows me everywhere. Every life I touch seems to be scarred after my impact. I don't care. I live my life for only two gods... myself and drugs.

I have no morality left in me. Sex is nothing to me, a game, a pawn, a way to make people my puppets... I don't know why. I'm very good at it, and I know it.

My last lover was HIV positive. I truly in my own way loved that person. They tried to talk to me about God, but I laughed at that ridiculous notion. Where has God been in either of our lives? It was a moot conversation to me... there was no loving God.

My mom had been sick for a long time also. She was in rehabilitation hospital for two years. I watched as a sick serial killer slowly etched and ebbed her life from her. In all my darkness, my mom was the most beloved to me. I couldn't help but to cry when I saw her. When she would pass, I believed it would be the end of what little humanity I had left in me.

God started working on me at this time.. When I would see an animal struck by a car, I would take them out of the street. One night or early morning around 2:00am or so, I was crossing a street and I saw a white cat. I went to it, and picked it up. It was still warm. When I got to the sidewalk, I realized it was still alive. I must have knocked on 20 doors trying to find its owner. I didn't want the cat to die alone, so I went back to it. I tried to comfort it. Then out of the blue, it started purring. I had heard that cats do not voluntarily purr. They purr only when they are happy or content. The purring started out softly and grew louder and louder until it was the loudest purr I had ever heard. Then I saw the light grow dim from its eyes, and it had moved on.

Around that same time, a friend had a major stroke at his job. He lay comatose, and the doctors had pronounced him brain dead. A friend and I went to the hospital to say goodbye. The next day the family was going to take him off life support. Denise couldn't bring herself to go in, so I ended up going by myself. As I sat in that room looking at him, he looked so peaceful, so gothically beautiful. I started doubting my old beliefs, the agnostic views, and the atheist ones. These four events had a tremendous impact on my mind and heart.

One day I was sleeping in a park. I got a message

telling me my mom was moving to Texas. I got on my bike and rode across town to her. I thought she was leaving that day. I was panicked. When I saw her she looked very ill. She needed me, and I was so strung out. We talked and agreed that if I could stay straight, I would follow her to Texas, take classes and be her caregiver. We had this conversation of me being her caregiver numerous times before. I always got high and would be out of control. This time it was different for me. I had been thinking of how long my mom would be around, and wondered if when she died there was there really a heaven? Could I really be with her again? So I started the process of getting back on my psyche meds and getting back into mental health housing. I had to stay at the mission, and stay in the Salvation Army. My mom supported me emotionally and financially. I later realized that she spent her rent money for me to have a place to lay my head. I started going to church at Salvation Army a little. This was the second time I got back in the mental health program, so I already knew Reverend Ron and his wife Leslie. My mom ended up having to leave the rehabilitation hospital. Even though she never told me, to this day I believe it was because she helped me to pay to have a bed to sleep in until I got back in mental health. She left for San Antonio, and three days later she got sick and died. I was devastated; I had a lot of people praying for me. I ended up getting high again, and left the program. I hit a new low doing both meth and cocaine. I was at a half-way house, and I had spent all my rent and food stamps on crack. No one could help me with the money. I was so depressed that all I wanted to do was die. I really contemplated suicide. Then I got on my knees and I prayed. From my heart, tears flowed, and I knew that I needed God. And He listened and answered. I called a number to a ministry in Houston, Texas, and without even knowing me, they sent me a bus ticket to come from Las Vegas. Only God could make this happen.

When I got there it was harder than I thought it would be, but I kept myself in the word to get by. The harder the days, the more I read and the more I prayed, so the closer I became to God.

God had restored my relationship with my estranged brother. I told him of the difficult time I was having, and he helped me get to Austin, Texas. I stayed at the Salvation Army Safe Sleep Program there, and my brother helped me get a seasonal position with a lifeguard company. I had met some very good ladies down in Austin, but JoJo and Beauty were my closest friends. Beauty took me under her wing, and we kept each other lifted up and stayed plugged in with church. JoJo was my spiritual friend, a full-blooded Indian.

My time limit was just about up at Salvation Army, so I was in the process of going back to Las Vegas when a friend from the Houston ministry told me about New Beginnings. She had left Houston, too. At first I wasn't too keen on the idea because that last ministry was very trying and hard. I didn't want to relive that, but she told me this was unlike any other place she had ever experienced. I told her I was going to Vegas, and she asked me why. I told her I had some legal matters to clear up. She said, "That's crap, you're going to get high." And you know what? She was right. So I called Missy at New Beginnings, and she let me come.

In the last ministry I was always afraid of being kicked out, and I had the same trepidation when I got here. I was a mess, as I was weaning myself off of some heavy psyche meds, and my mind was confused. I had huge trust issues. Also, my heart was still broken.

Missy pulled me to the side and told me, "Anne, you do not have to worry about being kicked out." I had never told her I was worried about that, she just sensed it.

New Beginnings has helped me deal with a lot of issues I have. I still have issues, but I'm making progress.

I have totally changed from the person I was before. The love and kindness I get here has been LIFE CHANGING.

Coming here, or better yet, God placing me here has been a life-changing event. The women here are great, and when I tell people about New Beginnings, I always hear what my friend told me come from my lips. This is not like any other place I have been. This is a home, a new way of life. I'm grateful for all God has brought me through. For saving me, and for being there when I didn't even realize it. For being the father I always wanted. I thank Jesus for making a way for me, for loving me even when I couldn't love myself, and making it possible for me to be able to be with my family reunited in heaven. I'm also grateful for MISSY giving me the chance to come and for the guidance and mentoring that I needed, and especially for loving so many of us when we couldn't or didn't know how to love ourselves or others. She has sacrificed more than we know, she and her family. I love that woman.

I also tell people that the past doesn't define who you are. The past can refine whom you become if you take heed of your mistakes and try and learn from them. We are all new creations.

I still will never be the mother of the year, or those other things I first mentioned, but I am also not that same person I told you about. Praise God.

Anonymous

Some prayers are unanswered, but He blesses those who believe. So, I am sitting on the couch just kicking back thinking of all the blessings God has bestowed upon me. I got out of jail October 13, 2013. Signed for seven years probation, and I believe with all my heart that God will walk me through it all.

While being in jail, God did test my faith. Let me explain. I was sitting in jail swearing up and down that I was going to prison for a while. I was scared, but I would pray and pray for God to do what He saw fit for me. After I prayed that prayer, I started having dreams about probation. I had this dream more than once. Another thing I was praying about was to go to Missy's New Beginnings program.

A couple days before I went to court, Missy talked to me. I told her about the dreams I had, and that I had them more than once. I told her that they couldn't be a coincidence, and that I believed it was God. She most definitely agreed.

After talking to her, I went back to my cell. That night, I heard the number "seven". At the time, I didn't know what it meant. I was thinking, "Seven years probation or prison?"

Finally, my court date came. When I went to court, my attorney said, "The prosecutor is offering you seven years probation!" I was so excited! Then I realized that was what "seven" meant! God was working miracles! I could feel Him in me and around me. All I could say was, "God is so good. He is awesome!" I looked at my friend and said, "God does answer prayer!"

But there was a twist to my case. The day before I went to court, they came at me with a Class A Misdemeanor. The stress returned, but I still believed God had it under control. And He did. I sat in jail for three extra days because the day I went to court, they were dismissing it.

On a Monday, I got to misdemeanor court to find that they still didn't drop the case. Back to holding I went. So I was sitting in the holding tank, bawling my eyes out when out of nowhere, God was telling me not to cry because He had it under control. Then I was pulled from holding, and the sheriff lady was standing by her car with a big smile. She asked me, "Do you want some good news?" Of course I said, "Yes!" She said, "The case has been dismissed, and you're going home!"

I am writing this to the ones who think the worse, like me. But the message is, "When all feels rough, turn to God. He's got your back!"

--Anonymous

Betty

My name is Betty, I am 54 years old, and I'm starting a new life. I give thanks to New Beginnings for this chance. I arrived here in May 2011, because of my lifestyle and choices I had made. I lost my freedom, and had been incarcerated.

Upon my arrival here, I felt this is what I have been looking for all my life. God has touched me and has been in my heart since the day I walked through the front door. Missy is my angel that glows with the love of the Lord. She and New Beginnings have shown me a better way to live. I have seen miracles and the

Lord's work every day. Not a day passes that I don't give to the people who have made these things possible. This house is truly God's house, and through Him nothing is impossible. I know this first hand because I am proof of what God's love can do when you let Him in your heart. It's because of New Beginnings and Missy that I have been given another chance. My faith grows stronger every day. When I see people give of themselves for this home so that a woman like me can have a place to stay, a roof over their head, running water, and food on the table, I know that is the Lord's work. He is working through others. I give praise to Jesus, and thank Him each day for the people who care for this ministry, and for Missy's vision and dream coming true to help those who want a better life, to have God in their hearts, and to have a "NEW BEGINNING." (August 2011)

Betty (Continued)

I came to New Beginnings to change my life where no one knew me or my past for a fresh start, a new beginning. But I needed someone to give me that chance. That person was Missy Denard. She was willing to give me that chance. This began my journey with Christ. I didn't know what to expect or do, all I knew at that time was this was where God wanted me. If God wanted me here, I knew He had my back.

Upon accepting Christ, a tremendous weight was lifted off my shoulders. My heart was filled with the love of God!

It hasn't been easy. There have been tough times when evil has tried to take me back. I have left and come back; I have fallen and made many mistakes, but through it all, Missy has been there for me.

Now that I have been here for a while, I believe God has me here for a reason. That reason may just be to help other women who pass through these doors who feel alone, worthless or unworthy of God's love. It might be to be a witness that with God in their life, anything is possible, or to share the miracles I have seen Him do for others and for me. There is a reason our paths cross even though we may not know it now. Each and every one of us take something and leave something else with each other. As I help others, it also helps me, and brings me closer to the Lord.

I am a work in progress. Being at New Beginnings has helped me regain my self-esteem, to be proud of who I am, and to be grateful for all the little things life has to offer. My relationship with my family has been restored. I am working on being independent, not to fear the outside world, to trust others, have forgiveness, and to show grace and mercy like they have been given to me. With God and Missy both by my side, I know I can do this.

Missy believed in me when no one else did, including myself. Her love for us is unconditional. There are times when Missy puts us before herself. When you look at her, you see Jesus in her. Her faith in Him is so great. To me, Missy is my mentor and family, but most of all, my friend. (Summer 2014)

Casey

Growing up, my life felt and even looked like a disaster on the inside. Whether it was inside my house or just inside my mind, everything was out of control. I remember when I was about four or five years old, I laid eyes on my dad for the first time. He had just stepped out of prison, and he wanted me to stay a night with him; and I was frightened. Never did I imagine that this fear would last what seemed like a lifetime. My mom was with my uncle at the time of my dad's incarceration. I only have a few memories while she was with him; he was very abusive. He would pin my older sister up against the wall by her throat while my mom just stood in fear.

After a while, when my dad was released on parole, my mom got back together with him, and every day turned into a bigger battle. My dad controlled everything we did. He was an alcoholic. Looking back on my life now, I can see where God's hand was on me because He saved my life. We would always go searching for my dad at some bar, and when we would find him, my mom would be driving us home while my dad was drunk in the passenger seat. Before we knew it, he would want to drive, and he would try to grab the steering wheel from my mom while all four of us kids were in the back seat screaming with fear. It was a nightmare, but even more than that, it was my life. It was only through God's grace that we survive it each and every time. When we would arrive home, they would still be fighting, but then they would go after each other with a knife or rolling on the floor with their hands around each other's necks. By the time the fight was over, my mom would be so tired of it, she would try to end her own life. She was very suicidal, and as kids in the house, we would have to take the role of the parent and try to protect my mom from herself.

When my parents weren't around, my siblings and I took our anger that we had for them out on each other. We found ourselves doing the same thing we saw them doing, such as going after each other with knives trying to take each other out.

My dad gave me my first drink of alcohol when I was seven, and he started sexually abusing me when I was eight. Not long after that, his best friend started abusing me, also. I was so confused I couldn't tell my mom because I didn't want to see what the outcome would be. I had all these things running through my mind until one day everything just went numb. I felt as if I had no emotion to any of it.

The abuse went on for many years, and the more my dad would abuse me, the more I would drink. My sister and I would throw parties after they left, smoking weed and drinking anything we could find to ease the pain.

My older sister got kicked out of the house when she was thirteen for releasing the anger she held in for my parents on my mom, but my other older sister and I were close. At the age of thirteen, I had enough and I started running away. I went on the run with a girl from school only to find out I would be running for a long time. I ran away again when I was 14 years old, but this time was different because I was so desperate to stay away from my parents that I jumped in a car with a guy I didn't know only to be raped, and went home only to be called a liar. I found out that night my sister found a new family, and my parents agreed it was best if she lived there with them.

By this time, I felt as if I were alone, broken hearted, and lost. I didn't know where I belonged in this world, so I kept searching. I kept running. One day while I was on the run, I met a homeless man. He told me he would come right back, and when he returned; he had a lot of tools with him. He asked me to help him clean them, and after I did, he left once again and then returned. He pulled out a pipe and taught me how to use it. I first smoked crack at the age of 14. I was never really fond of it, but it helped ease the pain I had in my heart for the moment.

I always had my parents and the cops right on my trail as they had tried everything to keep me at home. They had put me on house arrest and in JDC, but the fear inside me would not let me stay at home. There was a pain deep down I just couldn't explain to anyone.

When I was about sixteen or seventeen, my dad and I came to Abilene to drop my aunt and uncle off from Fort Worth where we lived. We got them home safely, but the way back was a nightmare. I could always tell when my dad was drinking, and he definitely was. He thought we were almost home, but he couldn't have been more wrong. We were supposed to be headed toward Fort Worth, but ended up on a dirt road in Sweetwater. He was driving 100 miles an hour on a dirt road when I told him I had to use the restroom. I got out, and he drove off leaving me miles away from home. I had to call the cops to pick me up until someone could get there. They found him on the wrong side of the highway with his passenger side of his truck bumped up. This was another instance of God's grace in my life. Because he was on parole for forty years, he went back to prison.

After that, I moved in with my grandfather. That's when things really went down hill for me as I was abusing my grandfather by stealing his pills (Oxytocin and Valium) to the point that his doctor wouldn't see him any longer. This caused APS to follow my every move. I would drink until I would black out and wake up in jail.

I was truly a lost sheep. I felt a lot of shame in my life. I blamed everything that had happened to my family and me on myself. I didn't care anymore. I wanted to die, and on many occasions I tried to end my life just as my mom had; and I was being the same addict as my father. My grandfather found me trying to hang myself. I ended up in a Wichita Falls state hospital. I felt as if I had no purpose, and if this was my purpose I wanted nothing to do with it.

My grandfather begged me to go get help, and after a while I agreed. So I went to some rehab in Fort Worth that didn't last very long. I finally found a place in Abilene, Texas called the Serenity House. It took thirty days for me to get a bed, but as soon as they called, my grandfather was more ready than I was. We headed out the next day, and I made sure I took plenty of pills with me. As the trip went on, I had talked my grandfather into buying me liquor, and he would give me his pills on top of it. Not knowing, I kept asking him to stop by the store just so I could go in to the bathroom, and I would snort my own bag of pills. I woke up in the hospital two days later with tubes down my throat. I had overdosed and stopped breathing. After I recovered, I was escorted to the Serenity House, which became my home for the next thirty days.

After I got out, I moved to a place called the Noah Projects, but I knew something was missing and that it wasn't the place for me. I moved out, and went and live at a Baptist camp. I had never really heard about God, but I knew they were praying. I just didn't know what for or why because it had never been explained to me.

It didn't take long before I was on the run again. I moved in with a guy I had met at the rehab center just to return to my old habits. He treated me like I was nothing, and threw me out. I moved in with my aunt just to get kicked out for stealing her weed. Then at last I tried moving in with my mom, but that didn't work out at all. I had been trying to call out to her to let her know what happened, but by this time she was with my dad's best friend and I wanted to hurt her, so I went after her. I got tackled down by the police and kicked out.

I decided to move back to Abilene, Texas. I was going back and forth, and I honestly had no idea who I was or what my life was going to be. I didn't know what love was, but I was trying to find it. If someone was willing to show me even just a little bit of love, I was going to run with it.

I moved in with my aunt and her kids; but after not even two days of being there, she introduced me to this guy, and I moved in with him. I was still drinking, and smoking crack and weed. After about two months, this guy accused me of cheating on him and left. I stayed with my aunt again. I found out that CPS was after her. When she told me they were closing her case the next day, we stayed up all night smoking crack and drinking. That same night, the cops tackled me down and pepper sprayed me before arresting me.

That's when I met Missy Denard. She told me she had a place for me, and I agreed. I stayed in jail for a while. After a while, I was told I was pregnant. I sat in jail thinking and asking myself if I could do it. I had so many different emotions going on inside me that I didn't know what to think. I got released from jail and moved in with Missy, but my head wouldn't let me stay.

I went back to my aunt's house only to find her gone. The only person I had left was the baby dad's brother. So I stayed there. After a while I went to go get a checkup and I found out that the baby died at eight weeks. So I went into surgery. After I went back to where I was staying, I started drinking again and smoking weed. I got to the point where I couldn't take anymore, and I called Missy. She came over to pray with me bringing her "Jesus crew" with her. That's the night I heard the most beautiful song of my life.

The next day I showed up on her porch with all of my stuff. I knew in my heart I wasn't going to stay, and that I had to get out of Abilene. Missy agreed and called a friend she knew in Dallas who owned a house for women. She had taught me a lot about God, and had helped me heal from past hurts, but I still wasn't ready to change, so I ran off every chance I got. I overdosed on heroine and eventually got kicked out. I so desperately wanted to stop running, but I just couldn't stay in one place. I was just waiting to be let down; and if they weren't going to let me down, I was going to do it myself, and so I did.

I moved to another house in Dallas and actually stayed there for six months. I was so proud of myself, and I knew God was, too. Until one day when it all came crashing down on me. I ran again and moved in with a guy I barely knew. I was smoking weed and listening to music with him and trying to fall asleep. All of a sudden I heard a voice. I knew I wasn't going crazy, but at the same time I wasn't sure. This voice was telling me to go home. It said it over and over again. I sat up making sure I wasn't just dreaming. Then I laid back down ignoring the voice. That's when it got louder saying, "Go home my lost sheep." That's when I knew it was God. I laid back down ignoring the voice again. I woke up the next day and went to work trying to make everything seem normal, but in my heart, I knew it wasn't. I went back to this guy's house when I got off, and we decided to go out. We went to the bar and drank as much as we could, and then we left. This voice that I had heard the night before was still echoing in my mind. When the guy I was with wanted to go buy ecstasy, I couldn't do it. I knew this life wasn't for me anymore.

I then called Missy, again, and we talked. I love Missy with all of my heart. There is just a spirit of joy in her life that attracted me to her. I felt safe around her. I went back to the house I was at before, but things just still didn't feel right to me. I felt something was missing, and no matter how much I tried to make myself like it there, I just couldn't do it.

I prayed to God and asked Him to show me if this was the place for me. I prayed that if it wasn't where I was supposed to be to have the lady throw me out. That night when I got home, she told me to leave. That's when I called Missy. As soon as she showed up, I knew it was the right thing because I felt a peace like I hadn't really felt before.

I found a job the first week I was at New Beginnings, and now I'm getting ready to go back to school. I am comfortable with all the women here, and I know without a doubt that I have a family now that I can trust.

I have been healed from so many things that have happened to me in the past. I had lost myself in a world that was driven by the enemy. I didn't know what it was like to live a peaceful life without pain. I can tell you that the pain from a broken heart and a disconnection from God are the worst feelings in this world, but once you find the peace that you have been searching for, you can never run from it. I have tried and tried to run from His truth, but had no luck just more love.

Seeing what God has done for me in the past two years has been a remarkable thing. I don't have a fear of people like I did. He has shown me I can't put my trust in anyone like I do Him. Since then, I have let my expectations of others fade away. I have made it possible to love others past the pain and hurt. I still have many things to work on when it comes to forgiveness, but I know with my heart that God will guide me when I am strong enough.

My testimony doesn't even come close to explaining how much Missy has helped me or even saved me from myself. I am so blessed to have someone there to help me find my way closer to God. Missy is my best friend, my guardian Angel, and my mother. Thank you, Missy because you were faithful to God; you have helped save many people. You are a blessing, and I love you.

Cherissa

New Beginnings has changed my life. It has given me a second chance, a place with hope and the fulfillment of love in Christ Jesus. Being in a 22-year addiction and just stepping out of prison, I knew I had to make a change. Missy Denard opened the door of New Beginnings to me. Given this chance, I felt a security that gave me the confidence to be the person I am today. I have been clean and sober for over two years now. The Lord has blessed me with a joyful spirit and determination. I no longer doubt my salvation. I am honored and grateful to be a part of New Beginnings.

Cindy

I remember when I was seven my daddy left. I didn't know why or where, just that he wasn't there anymore. I was the oldest, and the only girl. My dad was my world, my everything. I was heart-broken, and just could not understand why he wasn't there.

My mom remarried, and so my step-dad raised my younger brother and me. He drank a lot, and didn't show us any kind of love, only a lot of negative verbal abuse. I didn't know he could show any love at all, until my half-brother was born, and then it was still shown only to him.

I left home with my mom and step-dad at sixteen and went to live with my dad and step-mom. She was jealous that my dad had a wife and kids before her; so that didn't work out very well either.

I met a man who became the father of my oldest son. I knew him three weeks. We got married and pregnant three months after that. We started drinking, smoking pot and tried speed a couple of times. Mostly we were drinking at that time. I was constantly depressed. I didn't know anything else. When I drank, I wasn't as shy, and I felt like I was someone else who was more outgoing and happy, at least I thought that at the time anyway.

After that marriage, I realized that he was not the man. I got with another man, and was with him for seventeen years. We had a son and daughter together, and raised my oldest son as well. This is when the real drug use got started. Off and on for the most part of my life, I have used drugs and alcohol.

I raised my children their whole lives as a drug addict. The kids' dad and I split up finally after all those years of abuse. In our addiction, we were verbally abusive to each other. There was physical abuse as well, and a lot of hurt.

I found a third husband along with more drug abuse and more hurt. This husband and I learned how to make our own drugs, so it became easier to stay high, and easier just to become unhappy and lost in a horrible addiction.

It became so bad, for so long, I lost who I was, and didn't know anything. There was despair, depression, and hurt.
We got caught up in the drug world so deeply that it was both a miracle and a relief to get caught and go to jail.

I had been praying for God to do something to change the way things were. "I couldn't do it anymore!" He and I both went to jail, but somehow, I knew things were going to get better.

This was when I met Missy. I went to church in jail every time we had it. I read out of my Bible, and most of all, I prayed as much as I could. I knew the Lord, and I had a relationship with Him off and on since I was a kid. My grandparents were Pentecostal. I got closer and closer to Him. He gave me peace, hope, and blessed me all the time. I stayed in jail for four months, waiting to see what they were going to do with me. My charge was aggravated possession of over 70 grams of methamphetamine. My bond was $101,000, so I knew I wasn't getting out anytime soon.

After about three months, I asked my lawyer to set a court date for me for bond reduction, because I wanted to be on the outside work crew. The judge talked to me on the stand. Before I realized what happened, he lowered it to $10,000! I was out on bond the next day on a CRSP Bond "WOW!" The Lord had His hand in that, no doubt! I came to New Beginnings and stayed four months. I got closer to the Lord every day, and was on the right track. Missy taught me a lot. "I love her so much!" However, I left New Beginnings and got back with my third husband only for him to desert me again. I was devastated and felt like I wanted to die. I was hurt so badly. We had started using drugs again. Finally, I called Missy and she came to another town to get me. She took me back to New Beginnings. I am now doing really well! I have two jobs and great friends.

I am now trusting the Lord and getting my relationship back with Him. The blessings and love He is pouring out on me are awesome! I have peace in my heart, and people I can count on and trust.

Thank you Father for your healing, love, forgiveness, and Grace!
Thank you Missy, for not giving up on me!

Clarissa

I don't remember when the sexual abuse began. I'm sure it was much earlier than I can remember. Fourth grade is when I do remember it; when I knew something was wrong. It lasted until I was in the sixth grade. In the meantime, my step-dad's nephew sexually abused me every time he babysat my brothers, sisters, and me. I couldn't have my friends over to the house because of the way he would stare at them, and the things he would say when they were gone; so I finally quit having anyone come over.

My parents fought a lot, and they abused us all physically and mentally. They called me a whore, but I wasn't! I never remember my mother telling me she loved me; and I always wondered why.

I started smoking pot, drinking, and sneaking out at night. I got into a little trouble and got married early just to get out of the house. This was a big mistake! He was not better. He beat me for no reason. After a while, he didn't tell me he loved me, either. My boys were the only great things that came out of that marriage. After ten years, I finally left him. I married three more times after that, and they either cheated on me or stole from me.

I started using cocaine at age 38. That lasted for 15 years. I had horses, cars, jewelry, and kids. Then they were all gone.

I was in prison three times. This last time I was in jail, I met Missy Denard. She was teaching Life Skills classes; teaching that even though we've fallen short, our God and Jesus loved us, and would never give up on us.

Missy gave me a home to go to when I got out. She was and is my friend, mentor, and mom. If it were not for Missy and New Beginnings, I would be out on the streets, higher than a kite and still stealing for my habit. Because of New Beginnings, I have a home to always come to, and a new life with my Heavenly Father, and Jesus!

I love Missy so much, and I am so thankful that I found her.
She never gave up on me!
Clarissa

DeAnna

I have been broken and lived in deep despair for many years. I have been physically and mentally abused since the age of sixteen by men and woman, who felt the need to hit me or bring me down a notch or two. I did not have any comfort in my life. I turned to drugs in 1997, and this gave me comfort and the "feel good" feeling that I had not had in my life. I've had my heart broken so many times by so many individuals.

After so much of that, I became angry and tired. There just wasn't any hope left. I found myself in prison time after time for a total of nineteen years. I was behind a drug addiction that was slowly killing my spirit.

Then God came into my life, after stepping out of prison the last time. He had a plan for me. My ideas were not His ideas. I was supposed to parole to a man I had been writing. When I was released, I called from the Fort Worth bus station, but this man was in jail. I thought, "WOW! What am I to do?" I was in a dilemma and knew I was on my way back to prison because I had nowhere to go.

God put it into my heart to call Missy Denard at New Beginnings. I kept arguing with God, "She won't accept me. Why should she? I'm nobody! I'm a failure!" In the end, I did call Missy. She came and got me at the bus station, and she went with me to the parole office the next day.

Missy accepted me; she didn't care if I was worthless. She took a dirty stone and polished it, worked with it, and made me a sober, clean woman! She told me how God loves me, and that she does too!

I wouldn't trade my many months at New Beginnings for a million dollars! With God and Missy to guide me, I now have my own home.
I may be broke all the time, but I'm so rich in love, and all of that is more important to me than any material!

Thank you so much, I couldn't have done it without God and Missy.I love you, Missy Denard, and don't ever forget it! You and God loved me when no one else did.

Jamielou

First of all, I have to say I am so blessed to have my parents. They are wonderful people who did their best to raise me right. What I did was on me and me believing what the devil told me.

All of us have a testimony and every one of them is worth telling. God wants us to help one another heal by sharing them, so here is a bit of mine. I pray that it will inspire and strengthen your faith in God's love and power. He has always protected me from extreme harm. More than once I put myself in the path of a "train" and walked away with only a few scrapes and bruises. He loves me that much, and I took it for granted. The devil kept telling me that I wasn't worthy, and I believed him.

This journey to know God and His word started with a true broken hearted prayer when I was in Louisiana. It took another three years for me to get back to Texas. I lived in San Angelo, Texas, at the Salvation Army for four months while still drinking and using any kind of drug I could get. I started using heroin at that time, too. I paid them every two weeks for a bed while I was working for Labor Ready.

On Saturday, May 11, 2013, I woke up with no money to pay for the night. It was the first time I would have to sleep outside, and I was scared. I wasn't going to ask my parents for help because they had already done enough for me. I went to Labor Ready praying

138

they would have something for me. They did, and at the end of the day, I was sharing my situation with the lady I had worked with. She told me about the home she lived in, and gave me the number to call. When I did, I was invited to live there.

During that time, I was still using and even had the house parents taking me to the ER. Four months later, the house had to close. One of the women knew Missy and asked her if I could go to New Beginnings to live. Thank God she said yes. So once again, I was on the move. However, this time, God was going to make sure I stayed because this was where He wanted me to be.

My life was almost like watching a movie with God as the awesome director and me as the headstrong actress. I wanted my way when His is truly much easier. I've had to let go of my will and be obedient to Him and those in authority over me even at work. It's been rough because I was so used to having my way. I know I've been spoiled. I've fallen a few times, however, instead of doing what the devil expected me to do, which was run away, I faced him with God's strength and the blood of Jesus.

There are still moments my flesh wants to take over, and there may be times when it does. However, I know I must read my Bible, apply it to my life, and live it out everyday.

Jessica

My name is Jessica. I am 22 years old. In 2009, I lost my children. My dad who had raised me got very sick and became a very bad addict. He was diagnosed with Syphilis, Diabetes, and Hepatitis C. He is now going blind and has hallucinations. I also became a very bad addict; we were using together. We drifted apart, and I was living on the streets alone because he was so caught up in his addiction that he left me to fend for myself. I had never been on my own before, and I can honestly say that the streets are something I never want to experience again. Things were so very hard. The man I once knew as my father had become a monster in front of my own eyes. He used to be my hero. I love him so much, but it's time to let go and let God. I can't help someone who doesn't want to help himself.

When I met Missy in 2010, she could see that the spirit within me was lost, and I cried out because it was very hard for me to find my place in this world. The first night I met Missy, she was doing church at the jail, and I went. I told her my name, and she said, "You must be the girl your lawyer was telling me about. I have a bed for you, and can't wait to have you!" When she looked at me, it was obvious she could see the hurt and loneliness I was going through. She said, "You're not alone anymore!" She has stayed true to that. I love her! She is the mom I have always prayed for; I always wanted, but never had.

She has a passion for what she does for us girls. She was the angel in my darkness.

The journey I have been through was no easy road. I have experienced some things that are unexplainable. I finally opened up and was able to discuss those things with her, and for once in my life I wasn't judged for the things I did or went through. I've learned that we have to struggle in order to be the people we are to become. I was a single caterpillar when I started to become a Christian. Now I am being transformed into the beautiful butterfly God intended me to become.

Four months after coming to New Beginnings, I had to leave because I messed up. I have learned to be strong and trust in the Lord, and I know that He will make my pathway straight.

I came back home on December 10, 2012, after spending 11 months in prison. Missy was very welcoming. She made me feel comfortable with the person I am. I know now where I belong after all the hard times and struggles I had to go through. It has taught me some things such as to never give up on myself, to have the courage to face the things of this world, but hold on to what you have. Beauty will get you nowhere, and strength is the key.

I have been without my children for three years now, and I'm tired of living on the streets, not knowing if tomorrow will bring life or death. I don't have to worry about those things anymore!

Thank you, Missy, for your help, and for letting me know I am worth something. You're my inspiration! I know one day I will be the successful woman and mother God has called me to be. If I can change one person's life with my story, so their life doesn't have to be as complicated as mine was, then I have achieved something valuable.

The test to know if your mission here on earth is finished is, if you're alive, it isn't! I've learned that those who don't plan for the future have to live through it anyway. When you think you can't make it through, remember, I'm living proof that you **CAN!** Even if you're on the right track, you'll get run over if you just sit there. Just know you can succeed. Life is a beautiful thing. Learn to embrace it, and love yourself for who you are. **GOD LOVES YOU!**

May God be with you! Don't give up on yourself because you're worth it!
There's no need to follow when you can lead!

Kim

"And I am convinced that nothing can ever separate us from God's love. Neither death nor life, neither angels nor demons, neither our fears for today nor our worries about tomorrow – not even the powers

of hell can separate us from God's love. No power in the sky above or in the earth below —indeed, nothing in all creation will ever be able to separate us from the love of God that is revealed in Christ Jesus our Lord. Romans 8:38-39

My name is Kim Richardson Parks. I have known about God all my life, but I chose to live the way I wanted to, and that was not right. So I ended up in Taylor County Jail. It was not my first time, but it would be my last, thanks to an angel named Missy Denard. I found God again on August 9, 2008, in Taylor County jail. I was baptized October 9, 2008, in Taylor County Jail.

One day I was sitting in my single cell, and I was mad because I was there. Some of the ladies came by my cell and asked me to go to church. I told them I wasn't going to church in the world, so I wasn't going in there. But just before the cells closed, the Holy Spirit moved me, and I ended up going to church.

That night I met my angel, Missy Denard. As soon as I saw her, I started crying and she hugged me. She asked me if I would want to go to the Good News Camp, and I told her yes.

Shortly after that, I was sitting in my cell feeling very lonely because I didn't have any visitors or money on my books for a whole month. So I was crying and

143

feeling lonely, and I just started talking to God. I asked Him to hug me, and He did, and my life has not been the same since.

I left Taylor County Jail on the 6th of November that year and went to Fisher County Jail. Then the Lord blessed me, and I got out on November 26, 2008. I was supposed to go to the Good News Camp that Missy told me about, but it was closed for the Thanksgiving holidays, so I was blessed to be invited to stay with my "spiritual mother" and "spiritual dad", Missy and Rocky Denard and their lovely family for the holidays. I stayed with them for four days, and went to the camp on the 30th of November.

While I was at the Good News Camp, I was feeling lonely because I had not seen any of my family. I was asked to go to the Flying J, which was a truck stop with my sister and brother in Christ who were running the camp, Valerie and Scott to see their family. I went with them and met their daughter and son-in-law and kids. While we were there, I was playing with their grandchildren and talking to their daughter and son-in-law, and it made my heart hurt because I was missing my grandchildren, daughter, son-in-law and other family members. At that moment, I looked up and there was my uncle, Iria Ephriam, aka Bubba, walking out of the restroom. I had not seen him in two years or more. I jumped up and started running toward him calling his name. He turned around and hugged me, and I started crying. Before this, I would run from him because he was a man of God. I told him to go with me to meet my spiritual family, and he did. While we were talking to them, we saw more members of our family that we hadn't seen in a long time who were also living for the Lord. We praised Jesus and cried together, and then we all went our own way. I went back to the Good News Camp, whicht was a life-changing place for me.

I want to thank God first and my spiritual parents second, and of course the Goff family of the Good News Camp. I hope and pray that anyone who needs to find the Lord will look up Missy Denard.

I got married November 17, 2012, and I'm still living for our Lord and Savior, Jesus Christ. I will love God, Jesus Christ and the Holy Spirit always and forever. Amen! May God keep blessing my mom, Missy Denard in Jesus' name! Amen!

Machelle

My life was a complete wreck. I had lost my family, home, car and my sanity. I didn't know where to turn. I had been given a two-and-a-half year sentence in a women's prison. Life was hard, and I had given up. I was hopeless, defeated and lost! Another inmate in the facility I was in had been to New Beginnings. As she related her story to me about New Beginnings, I felt a ray of hope. Could this place help me? Was I capable of change? I wrote as soon as I was given the address, but received no response. Then I found out I had one week before my release. Still, I had no response. My sister called Missy Denard, the Director of New Beginnings, and my hopes soared because she had a bed for me!

Since being at New Beginnings, my life has changed. I now look at life with a new perspective. I have re-established a relationship with my children and family. Through Missy's teachings, I have learned that with God in my life, all things are possible. Today, I let God lead me through my everyday life, and guide me where He wants me to go. Today, I am successfully employed and a productive citizen. If not for New Beginnings, I don't know where I would be right now. Thanks to Missy Denard for having faith in me, and seeing what no one else could see. Missy has been, and still is, my mentor, friend, family and mom!

Stephanie

Stephanie came to New Beginnings ready to change, but she wasn't quite ready to let go in every area. She left and realized she still wasn't ready to be on her own, so she came back. While she seemed to be doing well, she was still struggling with her identity. I had a dream that she was at a hotel in room #218, and she came out with a towel around her, and there was a guy with her. I called her the next day and asked if there was anything going on, and told her about my dream I had the night before. She said she had been talking to her ex, but it was no big deal. Well, that night she left New Beginnings with her ex. She later told me they went to a hotel that night and they were going to put her in room #217. She told them, "No way!" Remembering my dream, she thought, "That is too close to the other one," meaning room #218 from my dream.

Stephanie ended that relationship and jumped right into another one that was equally as bad. She ended up falling back into old behaviors, which caused her to have violations while being on parole.

Several months passed before she called to ask if she could return to New Beginnings. I took her back. She stayed with us about a month until September 12, 2014, when I took her to her parole hearing. Since she had several violations, they ended up keeping her in jail that day. She was later transferred to ISF.

She's come a very long way, and the mighty work God has done in her goes without saying. She's been ministering to so many ladies while being locked up. It's been amazing to see how her whole attitude has changed. We are waiting for her to come back home and join us.

On October 13, 2014, I received a letter from Stephanie that encouraged me so much; I wanted to share the following:

"Well, I got moved to the back. It was a random move. Oh Missy, I was mad! I came in, and there was a lady that had just gotten moved out of the tank I was in for starting trouble. A lady that I prayed for God to take out of there, and then I get moved into the same tank as her. WHAT? So, I prayed and I prayed, and then Summer came to visit me the next morning. That gave me joy! I continued to pray about my issues with the lady. What came over me was..."Take yourself out of yourself and share the love and the word of God!" That's what I felt, and then God gave me Isaiah 61:1-2. Well, that's what He showed me. Missy, I truly in my heart feel that's another reason I am here. To share what I, myself have experienced, the love and forgiveness of God. Praise the Lord! It is an awesome feeling. I never would have thought I would be able to just call out and quote scripture to someone when they needed it, when it applied to their situation. We talk about God every day in here. Girls ask ME questions about Him! Today, one of the girls told me she was happy I got moved in here because of my positivity. Wow! God has given and shown me so much in just this last month. Even though I want to be home, I am thankful for that! AMEN!! He is definitely doing a work in me, that's for sure."

Love,
Stephanie

Summer

My name is Summer, and I have been to prison three times. I have lost everything so many times that that has been my norm. I have three boys, one of which I don't see, ever; honestly I don't even talk about him.

148

I don't know exactly where or when I went wrong. My home was nice on the outside. I grew up in a place in Wall, Texas. My mother was a nurse, and my father was a forklift mechanic. I lived on 20 acres of land, which was the American Dream, with three brothers and sisters. It looked like we had everything, but both of my parents were addicted to drugs. My mom was into prescription pain pills. I started with Darvocet, and then moved on to Meth. I was 15 when my dad taught me how to cook dope. Our lives just crumbled. We didn't even see it coming.

Before I realized it, I was addicted to both. I was using Meth to wake up and sneaking my mom's Xanax and Somas to go to bed. I would leave school early to go on pill runs. I did graduate, and I even got involved in a church to try to find a calm, but there was none.

When I was upset or uncomfortable, I just did more drugs. There were so many secrets. My mom had no idea what we were doing. She was always so busy or tired. My dad knew what he was doing; he just didn't care. My family fell apart. I moved out a bunch of times, and moved back a bunch of times as well.

I met the father of my kids and then I started cooking my own Meth because there just wasn't enough. He is doing 13 years behind bars; I have corrupted everything I have ever touched <u>until now!</u>

I don't know what the future holds for me, but during my last trip to prison, I stumbled onto NEW

BEGINNINGS, and I honestly had nowhere else to go. It has been the best thing that has ever happened in my life. I am not judged. I have so many demons in my life, but slowly I am coming to terms with the wreckage of my past, and I am using it to my advantage. I can smile, and I am not ashamed of who I am. I am getting to know the Lord and that would have never happened if it weren't for Missy! She is a beautiful woman, with a passion to help, and she has a way about her that you just can't get enough of. Before coming here, I was a broken, angry, bitter, evil person, and I cared only for myself. I now have a family again. I see my kids. I have an opportunity to help others before they wind up in my place. Missy made me see that life isn't evil. It's beautiful! Everyday we have an opportunity to reach for and see that we are worthy of another chance. With God's help, all things are possible. I have a yearning inside me to learn about life through the eyes of the Lord, and I see now what I can be.

So, thank you, Missy for giving me a chance! Without New Beginnings, I wouldn't have ever had the chance to <u>love me!</u>

*****UPDATE FROM MISSY*****

Summer has worked so hard to get her boys back. She never thought it was really possible for her. When her aunt told her the boys wanted to come live with her, she was so excited as well as nervous. They aren't just typical boys. They are special boys with special needs. Not only has she had to learn how to handle their medication, but she also has to keep up with the paperwork that has to be turned in to the state weekly regarding the approved list of people who help with her boys and the hours they spend with them.

For the first time in her life, Summer had a healthy relationship with her dad after he received Christ and gave God control of his life. However, just shortly after moving into Phase Four with her sons, her dad went to be with the Lord in Heaven. This was a very trying time for her because her life was full of new adjustments.

She has really blossomed as a mother. She works a full time job, cares for her two sons, takes them to doctors and counseling appointments, and still helps New Beginnings by talking with and encouraging the new ladies who join us. She gives back in amazing ways. Summer never had a mother, but she calls me "Momma", and that's a sweet blessing to me. I truly believe God has connected us in a special way.

Susan

My First Taste...
I remember my first taste of booze around the age of four. It was bourbon mixed with lemon and honey, to keep me from coughing....at first! I had it several

times as a child, and looked forward to the warmth of the drink and the peaceful sleep it brought.

My first illegal drug was at the age of sixteen. I smoked pot with my dad, who I only met six years prior. Mostly, it was just my mom and me and whichever man was currently in her life. I was molested early on by various family members. Mom's second husband molested me and raped my stepsister, his own daughter and got her pregnant. The third husband raped me for three of four years and beat my mom for seven years.

I drank a bit here and there, but mostly, I just did all I could to stay out of the house with school activities and working. I had become a pretty good "party-goer". I drank often and was the life of the party. By this time, a new man had entered mom's life, and I wasn't sticking around for that.

I moved 350 miles away to get to know my real father. We drank a lot together, used cocaine, and smoked a lot of pot.

That summer turned into winter, and there were new friends. In nine months, I learned more about drugs like ecstasy, LSD, and lots of alcohol. I got bored and joined the army. I had more time and money now to use various drugs, drink a lot, get into methamphetamines, and relationships with a lot of men and women. Alcohol was always my best friend, but I'd use whatever I had.

I have one daughter living, and one that I aborted. I hated myself so bad for so long, before I ever had my first child. Almost three years later, and already losing custody my first little girl, I decided to take my life so I could party on. I found that I loved crack cocaine and whiskey. After a failed suicide attempt, I went to the nut house a few times. My relationships mostly with women were violent and jealousy plagued me. I ended up losing jobs, homes, relationships, and had a few jail visits overnight. I sold and used Meth for years, but mostly I drank. I was just crazy enough for psych wards, and drank enough for six rehab visits.

I was diagnosed bi-polar, with anxiety attacks, post tramatic stress disorder, multiple personalities, severe depression, anti -social disorder and more. I took Xanax, Depakote, Zoloft, Prozac, Lithium, Librium, Trazodone, Seroquel, and many others. I prostituted for drugs for a while. I chose to be homeless so I could drink more. I almost killed myself in an accident from smoking and snorting too much ice.

I had forged some checks on my boss before he fired me. I retaliated by drinking and living on the streets before I turned myself in on the charges. I spent five and a half months in jail. While I was there, I prayed a lot, went to church, Alcoholics Anonymous, and Life Skills classes. That's where I met Missy Denard, and heard the voice of God. I began to recount the many horrid days I spent begging God to take my life on my knees, crying to Him, with a crack pipe in my mouth. Visions of near death experiences throughout my life poured over me in jail. God revealed Himself time and time again to save me from myself in countless situations, and all I had to do was acknowledge Him. He spoke to me through Missy, and told me to trust her. I was convicted for the first time, not condemned by the homosexuality lifestyle I had been in for eighteen years.

I came to New Beginnings broken and torn apart by satan's lies that consumed every part of my life and identity. I accepted Jesus Christ as my Lord and Savior. I am free of seizures, bi-polar disorder, and every other disorder placed on me by the enemy. I no longer take medication, and haven't for eight months. I am free of the spirit of homosexuality, although; remnants remain. I am free of the bondage of my parents, grandparents, men, and utter defeat. I am a new creation in Christ! I have a new relationship with my family, my daughter, and with myself. I love me today! Missy has ministered to me all hours of the night and day. She has held me when I wasn't loveable. Missy is such an encourager of people; she speaks the truth even when it hurts, and loves the way God intended it to be. She has shown me what the difference is between knowing of Christ and knowing Him personally. I am so thankful to Missy, but mostly to God for sending His Son to die for me!

*****UPDATE FROM MISSY*****

Susan is attending college at Hardin Simmons University working on her Bachelor of Behavioral

Science degree. She is extremely smart and is focused on bettering her life in order to be able to raise her 12-year-old daughter full time in the near future.

Mother of Us All

I don't think a lot of people realize what Missy does for us at New Beginnings, or the time she puts into us. I have called her at three, four, and five o'clock in the morning on multiple occasions because I needed prayer. I didn't have a personal relationship with Christ before I met her. I didn't know the enemy and his lies had me in bondage in so many areas of my life.

Missy and I have been through so much because of the anger inside of me. I have had victory after victory in Jesus' name because she loves me no matter what. She has held me when I was unlovable and has never backed down from the truth. I would give my life for her any day.

Missy may not please everyone with the way she does things, but I can tell you that she is very pleasing in God's eyes, and still teachable. He told me so.

But mostly, Missy is my friend and doesn't allow me to make excuses for myself. She has been a light in total darkness. "I love you" doesn't cover it, Missy. I can't wait to meet you in heaven and see what He has for you.

Susan
January 29, 2013

Veronica

Before I came to New Beginnings, I had tried since 2009, to stop the madness having realized that I was an alcoholic. I tried various ways to stop drinking. I went to numerous AA/NA (Alcoholics Anonymous / Narcotics Anonymous) meetings. I sought doctors and medication, and I had enough of all that, too. I became depressed, and thought I was no good to anyone, not even myself.

I had gotten my first DWI January 2010. My father was diagnosed with cancer with six months to live, but he only lasted three months. He was the only constant love in my life. At this point, I didn't think I could go on; so I took all the pills I had, and drank as much as I could. I fell asleep only to wake up three days later, and I knew it wasn't meant to be. I recognized that I had to fight and do whatever it took to get straight and off the alcohol. Well, with that came a lot of different emotions. I now realized I had been running for most my life. I know now I didn't know how to handle heartache, rejection, abuse, disappointment, and much more without reaching for that bottle to numb myself because it hurt so badly. I suffered a lot of physical and mental abuse, and I was also badly broken, but knew I had to find a way, "a right way", to cope and make it to Heaven to be with my father again. So, again, I sought out different ways to stay strong by attending counseling meetings, taking medications, and keeping busy, but I would continue drinking when things didn't work out. I had met a lot of different people along the way, and was in one more abusive relationship.

I was told I could stay with a man I fell in love with, but it turned out to be even worse. I was beaten, embarrassed in public, humiliated, isolated, and miserable; so I did the only thing I had control over, I drank. I decided while drinking that I had to leave which I did, only to get a second DWI. At that point, I went to jail on a Saturday. When I got out, I went back to the only place I knew which was "the old neighborhood." I thought I was strong enough to make things right and live with my old roommate when he told me he would help me until I was on my feet. Two days later, I found him passed out with a bottle of alcohol next to him. I had a hard day and thought "Just one drink, I can do this." I handled it well, I blacked out. When I woke up, I found him awake and wanting me to start a relationship. When I said no, he told me I had to go. I didn't know where to go, but I knew I couldn't stay there where I had to do something immoral to have a roof over my head.

So, I found myself homeless, but sober, frightened, hungry, and dirty. I got my sleeping bag and went into a tin shed I was renting from a person, and prayed the other guy wouldn't find out. Others saw me, but never told. I was there for over two weeks when finally, a friend who is more like a brother got me into a recovery house, and I thought it was the answer; and it was at the time. I was waiting to go back to court for my second DWI. I had to do 90 meetings in 90 days to stay at the recovery house. That's all they had to offer. Toward the last two weeks before I went to jail on an MTR (Motion To Revoke) because I was on probation, I was given so much wrong information from someone. This caused me to worry. She thought she knew what she was talking about because she had been running the recovery house. I was scared and confused. I could feel myself slipping, and knew something had to give. "It did!" A warrant came out for my arrest. I had to turn myself into jail.

I was very sick at this point. I was filled with pain physically and mentally. I was worse than ever with no relief, and sleep now became very hard. Just when I thought I couldn't take anymore, I went to church in jail, and I met Missy. I didn't think she was talking to me when she said, "I have a Transitional House, and offer help to anyone willing to call me!" I didn't even write her number down because I didn't even think she would accept me. I was released after 60 days, but on probation until June 28, 2013. I went back to the same recovery house because I had nowhere else to go, and it was worse than ever.

I had gotten to the point where I couldn't take it anymore. I bumped into a woman who had Missy's cell phone number and the address of New

Beginnings. I decided that I was going to call her. The day I got out of jail, my son who was 12 years old and living with his father in Fort Worth, was placed with CPS (Child Protective Services) there in Fort Worth. I couldn't wait to see him. "Thank God," I had put some money away, and was able to buy a round trip ticket to Fort Worth. I moved out of the recovery house, and went to Fort Worth only to find out that the day before (which was the day I got out of jail) he had been placed in their custody. Now, I was under their rules to see my son. Even though I had four months of clean time, they wouldn't let me have him. I came back to Abilene broken hearted and on the verge of relapse. I picked up the phone and called Missy, and left a message. I knew I wanted to stay sober and get my son back. I knew New Beginnings was where I needed to be. Missy and I kept missing each other, and the enemy was telling me she didn't want me, and that I'm not the type to get into a place like that.

I looked out the window, and there was a liquor store. I started thinking about drinking, and thought I could drink and just start over again in the morning. Just at that time, Missy called me and asked me to meet her in the morning, and she told me that I could stay at New Beginnings. I never looked out that window again. I left that following morning, and now because of Missy, I have been able to see my son every other week.

Although it's not always easy because shortly after moving to New Beginnings, I learned that the pain I had in my body was Fibromyalgia, Rheumatoid

Arthritis, and Hepatitis C. The good thing is there is a cure for Hepatitis C. Missy would pray about it, and sure enough, God answered my prayers. Today, my pain is less, and I'm able to function.

I get up every other Tuesday and catch the bus at 3:45am to see my son for two hours and then return to Abilene at 7:00pm. "Thank you Jesus!"

Because of New Beginnings, I have a relationship with God, and Jesus is my best friend. I know without a doubt that all things are possible through Christ. I also know I have a ways to go. With the support of New Beginnings and Missy, I know I can stay on track with no more reaching for alcohol or drugs to numb the pain. I know how to cope with what life has for me whether good or bad. I put God first and foremost. I still have issues I'm working on like going to see my son in California, who had a heart attack at age 32, but thank you Jesus that my mom and sister are there to help him. There have been so many blessings that it is amazing!

I am now working on getting a place of my own to bring my 12-year-old son home. I will always be a part of New Beginnings and the Bible class, Life Skills and events. I could never thank Missy and New Beginnings enough. Without them I would not know what hope, joy, peace and love are.
"THANK YOU JESUS!"

*****UPDATE FROM MISSY*****

The summer of 2012, God opened the door for Stephen to come home. I felt led to offer the back part of our first house to them since the second kitchen had been completed by this time, so Stephen could live with his mom. They lived there for two years, and have now found a place that suits them better. We continue to be a support system for her as she is dealing with severe health issues.

Vivanna

My name is Vivanna, and I came to New Beginnings on February 23, 2011. I have benefited greatly since I have been here. God truly gave me a new beginning when He brought me here to this house. I have grown a lot spiritually in the Lord. I know I have a strong foundation I can build on. I have learned to live by faith in every way, and to praise God through the good and the bad. I came to know what God's unfailing love is, and I feel and see God's power working in my life as well as in others who live here. I have also regained my self-esteem and know my own self-worth, "Who I Am in Christ", and that is most important of all. I have also learned how to live a clean and honest life. I learned how to walk through life and its trials and difficulties with grace, love, and compassion in my heart instead of hate, fear, and resentment.

I came here with just the clothes on my back, and now I have all that I need. God has truly provided for my needs through all those who have given donations to this ministry. I cannot thank you enough! I have also regained my relationship with my brother and dad while I have been here. I was also able to obtain my birth certificate and the other documents that I needed so I could get my ID. Now I can get a job and be successful. I was able to earn my freedom as well since I have been here. I successfully got through my probation and court hearings with Missy's help and support every step of the way. I am truly grateful! I appreciate all the prayers, donations, and support that have been given to this ministry. Through all that people have done, **I am a life that's changed!** God Bless You All.
Sincerely,
Vivanna

Life Skills Class
I Just Want To Thank You!

I just wanted to thank you all because you all listened to me, and you all would try to help me by using your own personal life experiences. No one was fake, and you all never judged me. We all opened up a little more and more with each class; and if only for an hour, we were able to **trust**, and for that I thank God.

In this class we have really been helping each other grow by learning ways to cope with past and present situations that have caused us to be angry, stressed, or even unable to love (especially our enemies) or be loved. My answer in these past weeks has been prayer. "Prayer from the heart," and **belief** in **all** our Lord Jesus Christ did for us then, and **Faith** in all He still does for us today. Not only do we have the works of Jesus from the Bible to tell us how to overcome trials and tribulations, But God has sent the Holy Spirit to walk us through them.

- **Psalms 34:4 "I sought the Lord, and he heard me, and delivered me from all my fears." (NKJV)**
- **Psalms 34:17 "The righteous cry out, and the Lord hears, and delivers them out of all their troubles." (NKJV)**
- **Psalms 32:5 "Finally, I confessed all my sins to you and stopped trying to hide my guilt. I said to myself, I will confess my rebellion to the Lord. And you forgave me! And all my guilt is gone." (NLT)**
- **John 16:13a "However, when He "the spirit of truth" has come; He will guide you into all truth." (NKJV)**

Grace and peace be with you always!

Life Skills Class

God Loves Me!

What I've learned is that **God loves me** so very much that He sent His son to die for me, and took all my sins. That fact is always with me.

In class, I've learned about stress. What I can do is to give it all to the Lord, take a walk, take a deep breath, talk to God like I'm talking to you, and I don't need to be negative because that's not from God.

I've learned to listen better to others, and this life isn't about me, it's about walking in love and serving others. I've learned about getting on my knees, worshipping, and praising God. Everything else comes in line: wisdom, knowledge, happiness, and joy. God doesn't give us more then we can bear. We shouldn't take it literally when someone gets angry and goes off on us. I see that a lot! When someone gossips through a lot of people, he is trying to hurt someone. I'm learning to pray them up because I know one of two things will happen, either the person will get better or they will get worse. Praise God! I trust in God, and I trust in His word. I thank Him for what He does every day, and for the things to come. God says, "Not to Worry." These things I have learned some from Life Skills class and from some books.

Thank you for being there for all of us. Missy, you are truly a child of God. I've learned the Holy Spirit is a gentleman; so I have invited Him into my life daily.

Your sister in Christ

Life Skills Class

Coping

Life Skills class is important to me because not only is it a privilege for me to get to attend, but it also helps so much to be able to understand each other better. It teaches us different ways to cope, bless, and forgive. It seems each day that goes by we go through so many different things.

Life Skills class helps me to get through a lot of things like feelings, misunderstandings, fears, or just anything. It seems like each time I attend class, I learn better ways to get along with my cellmates. We can now understand each other's different ways. The Life Skills class has taught me better ways to understand things. I learn a new lesson every week, and it seems like what we are studying that week is something I needed to learn right then. I can go and talk out the things that I am going through, feeling, or that has happened during the week. We can learn from these things, and eventually get through situations in a more positive way.

Life Skills Class

Confidence

Life Skills Class taught me how to address issues that I have, and how to share in a group openly and freely without feeling embarrassed and ashamed of not knowing everything.

I learned a lot from Missy. She is awesome, and has taught me that God has different plans for all of us, and we are all called to serve and minister in different ways.

God has brought us together because we share a lot in common. I enjoy talking to her. God uses her to speak to me. Missy makes the class worth attending. She is patient and very anointed, and God is surrounding her daily.

Life Skills Class

This Time Around!

I have learned so much this time around. First of all, that all the un-forgiveness in my life held me in bondage, and has been keeping me from having the relationship with Christ I was searching for. By shoving things down and not dealing with them, I was actually sinning! I had to turn it all over to Him, and then I was able to let go and forgive not only others, but myself!

I also learned that although I may not like the things someone does, I can love them through Christ. My bigger lesson came through Missy through her struggles and trials these last several months. She never wavered from her faith, and she never lost sight of God. Then seeing the blessing God has given her and her family following that time of trial was amazing! It has given me the hope and ability to hold my head up, and to see the light at the end of trials.

She is such a blessing to not only us, but also to God. She not only truly loves us, but she shares openly and completely. She gives us an example of how to love each other.

Chapter 10

"May the words of my mouth and the meditation of my heart be pleasing to You, O Lord, my rock and my redeemer." Psalm 19:14

~~~~~~~~~~~~~~~~~~~~~

In Life Skills Class, many women would write pomes for me. They would write whatever God put on their hearts. I have even had women who have gone on to other prisons write poems and mail them to me. These have been encouraging to me and to other women when I have shared them. By including them in this book, I know they will continue to bless even more lives as they reach more people.

A Letter From God to Women

When I created the heavens and the earth, I spoke them into being;
When I created man, I formed him and breathed life into his nostrils.

But you, woman, I fashioned after I breathed the breath of life into man
Because your nostrils are too delicate.
I allowed a deep sleep to come over man so I could patiently and perfectly fashion you.

Man was put to sleep so that he could not interfere with my creativity.
From one bone, I fashioned you.
I chose the bone that protects man's life. I chose the rib that protects the heart and lungs that supports him, as you are meant to do.
Using this bone, I shaped you, modeled you, "my beautiful lady!"

I created you perfectly and beautifully.
Your characteristics are as the rib; strong yet delicate and fragile.
You provide protection for the most delicate organ in a man.
His heart is the center of his being;
His lungs hold the breath of his life.
The rib cage will allow itself to be broken
Before it will allow damage to the heart.
You support man as the rib cage supports the body.
Because without you, man has no hope, no life.

You were not taken from his feet to be under him,
Nor were you taken from his head to be above him
You were taken from his side, to stand beside him
and be held close to his side.

You are my perfect angel.
You are, and will always be my beautiful little girl.
You have grown to be splendid woman of excellence.
My eyes fill when I see the virtues
In your heart, In your eyes.
Don't change them.
Your eyes are the eyes of compassion.
Your lips are the lips of truth. Your voice is the voice
of kindness.
Your heart is the heart of love.
I call you my sweet charity.
Your graceful hands are so gentle to touch.

From your womb, you bear the ultimate fruit;
Life is born from your womb, my beautiful life-giver!
I've caressed your sweet face in the deepest sleep.
I've held your heart close to mine.
I love to watch, you my divine, you are my palm.
You are never old, but you, like fine wine
Grow sweeter in time.
Of all that lives and breathes, you are most like me.
Hold your head up high
And please don't cast your pearls before swine.
Give me your praise; yes, don't ever stop praising me!
I've given you special discernment and special
intuition.

If man leaves you alone, I'll be by your side.

I'll never leave you!
Adam walked with me in the cool day, yet he was lonely.
He could not see me or touch me. He could only feel me.
So everything I wanted
Adam shared and experienced with me, I fashioned in you,
"My beautiful and special woman" because you are an extension of me.

"Who so findeth a wife findeth a good thing
And obtaineth favor of the Lord!"
Man represents my image; woman my emotions, even my thoughts.
Together, your spirit and man's spirit represents the totality of God!
Oh great woman of God, my beautiful bride, "I love you!"

So men, treat woman well!
Love her
Respect her!
She is fragile. However, without her you are nothing
Because she is that perfect extension of you.
Share this with all the women you know,
So they will always remember how special they are.
God loves all of you, woman!
You are God's wonderful creation

Calling Out

Jesus, I am calling out to you. Please give me strength. Help me through my day. My heart is heavy, and I am tired and weary. Sometimes, loneliness can carry much pain. Help me to see that this is the best way for me. I know that if I was focused on everything but myself, then I wouldn't be able to grow the way I should.

So I pray for peace, and ask peace be still and calm my waves. Give me reassurance that you are here every step of the way. My first and true desire is that I abide in you. I know to do that, there are things that I need to do, so I say goodbye to my yesterdays, and as they slip away I take your hand and obey; for my love for you is deeper than the ocean, and I am consumed by you.

You are my everything, and my full dependence is on you, so, at the end of my day, let me lay my head upon your chest and hear your heart beat, feel your everlasting arms around me, and know that you are God.

By: Vivianna

I am a Prison!

I am a prison; I'm damp and cold.
I hold women who are young, women who are old.
I'm surrounded by fences and gates that have locks.
My walls are made of sheets of tin instead of blocks.

I am a prison, and feared by all.
I'll give you a chill when you hear me call.
Your name becomes a number, your face just another.
I'll show you no pity, and I'm not your mother.

I am a prison designed to be rough.
I'm where society houses it's tough.
Nobody has beat me, though many have tried,
But mostly they all still remain inside.
I have no answers so don't ask me why
I put those tears in your children's eyes.

I am prison where no one wants to be
I confine women who were once free.
I control their pace, I slow down their stride,
I strip them of dignity, I take their pride.
Like animals you put in a cage
I contain women and watch them age.

I am a prison. I am full of despair.
I can be a woman's worse nightmare
I've been here many years, and will be many more.
You'll recognize me by my loud slamming doors.

I am a prison. A place you don't want to live.

I've so much to take, but nothing to give,
But there is One who does, and He hears your pleas.
So pray to the Lord Jesus, for He has the keys.

I Am Not The Same!

I am not the same
Since Jesus called my name.
I am that little girl always behind the alley being bad,
Because people always made me mad,
And now my face is so sad.

I'm not the same
Since Jesus called my name.
I'd run and hide and try to stay cool,
But every time I did, I'd just look like a fool.

I'm not the same
Since Jesus called my name.
In many alleys I lay, in many bottomless pits
Until the smell of blood came flooding
Through my veins.
I was in pain.

But I know that Jesus called my name,
And wouldn't let me down.
Because I am not the same
Since Jesus called my name.

So if the hard fall….
I was trying to stay out of jail,
And I'm a changed person,
Because Jesus called my name.

I was saved because it changed my way
So that when Jesus called my name,
I'm not the same

So today, look around
And hope I see the ground again
Because I had a dream
In that dream, I learned to love me.

I learned to love my Father
Because I am not the same,
Since Jesus called my name.
So, if you've been here,
It's time to call Jesus' name,
And He understands.
Be willing to receive
What He has to give.

The enemy will tell you
That if you surrender, it's easy.
But I'm not the same,
Since Jesus called my name!
I'm so glad to be back in the land of living.
I gave up and went back
To try to find that sack
I know I left it in that pack.
I would never find it
Because it was not mine

I've changed my way because
Jesus called my name.
So I understand what I need to do
Stay in the spirit of God the Father
Have His Grace, and always have his Peace.

So if you're locked up,

Or whatever you are,
Maybe just remember
That Jesus calls your name,
And you'll never be the same.

Someone might not know
What I am saying.
I am changed, my whole body and soul
Since Jesus called my name.

So if you'll just make a move to the right,
Jesus will see you in His sight
Because He is the light!
Like I am not the same,
Since Jesus called my name.
You will not be the same,
When Jesus calls your name!

Lesson Learned

A lesson learned, I have to say
As I stare at these four walls everyday.
I made some wrong choices and that's not ok,
But now God is helping me find my way.
I lost my friends and family, too
And only God knew what to do.

I prayed that He might show me the way,
And give me back my strength to fight another day.
It might not have been the way I thought it would be,
But Lord knows God is always right when it comes to me.

I found my way back into His arms, don't you see?
The sad thing about it is, He never left me.
I just lost my faith and no longer believed,
But He never lost His faith in me.

Jessica
July 2014

Lost In This World

Lost in this world, not knowing how each day would come or go.
"I live by Faith now; always to overcome what's brought in front of me."
The strength is given to me to be the woman God has called me to be.

"Heart and soul alone." I lived without love.
Not using my gift or even knowing I had one
Struggling each day to find my place in this world, I was killing myself with each day that passed.
I didn't know if I would live to see tomorrow.

Now God has me in the palm of His hand. Never to live again covered by the sins of my past, but to live as a witness to glorify my God: The one who washed away all of my darkness and brought me unto the light to continue the will He has written for my life.

Satan has no authority over me anymore. "I am a Child of God!" He will strengthen me by each step as I walk in faith.
"I am a chosen one to live amongst my brothers and sisters in Christ!"
We will work together to bring light in the cold dark world; to shine brightly to show God through us, and to help them have faith in themselves.

Someone once told me that just as we have faith in God; so God has faith in us. We can abide in Him so

He abides in us to give us eternal life! In His kingdom we will meet together as the congregation of Christ.

Missy

I saw the smile in her eyes when she opened the word, quieting uneasy spirits with the
Gentleness of her voice.

Yet not so still
For the spirit danced within her.... Roaring like a lion...

Unaware of hearts for Him she would embrace; eternity awaited those broken little girls.
She melted hearts of steel with teardrops and pouring from her healing prayers...

Boldly, with a whisper she requested entry into the darkness of souls, yet, untouched by
The freedom of His name.

By: Susan

O Child of Mine

O child of mine, listen to my voice, hear the call, feel the desire that burns from deep within your heart and soul. Feel the tingling excitement of your spirit as it feels my presence and hears my voice.

You know the voice of your shepherd. Take heed to it. Listen for my words are true, and they never fade away. The things I speak over you will not turn back void for they are the words of creation and life, just like the breath I breathe into you.

My love is real. Grasp it, take it, and run with it. Let it consume every part of you. Let it fill every wound, and when it has done that, let it overflow from you like a spring.

For what I have given you, there is no limit to…many things will come to pass for you, but keep your focus on me. Share in your joy by your praise to me. Child, "I love you!"

 And my love is ever unfailing, and will never end. So do not be afraid to surrender all of yourself to me. Come often and sit at my feet as you bask in my presence.

Abide in me, and I will make all things new, inside of you and all around you.

By: Vivanna

Reflections

I think of
All the things I've done
At the time
They were really fun. And now I reflect
I go all the way back.
Oh, My God
My life was black.

It was so black
That really couldn't see
See all the bad
Done to you, done to me.

God is now guiding the way
No left, no right
Just straight away

A chance to have
I will not fail
I'm going to heaven
Not hell!

On the right path
I will never veer
So let go, let God
And never fear. Never fear
That God is there
Get on your knees
Lay it bare.

Oh Dear Lord,
Forgive me of my sin
So one day I can finally win.

Win this game
I've played so hard
Trust in the lord
Play the right card.

Only with God
I can now win
I cast it all
All that I've been.

Unexpected Angel

I figured sex and drugs would keep me sane; I thought it could forever hide my old pain.

Only to wake and find it still creeping around; playing with my head, making the same old sound.

Stuffing the pain back deep within; my blindness kept me going back to the same old sins.

Only to be stopped by a divine intervention, being put with God in detention.

A time for me to learn to be still, God wanted me to see that He was real.

He put me in a place called jail. He made sure no one would make my bail.

In there he had sent me one of his angels; she was there to show me the right angles.

She had planted a seed in my heart, but it wasn't something I was willing to start.

Because I was full of so much fear, I wasn't ready to let God stir.

I got out and sinned all over again, Only for God to put me back in.

God wasn't going to give up on me, because of what I couldn't see, He had already had a plan

Even when I ran he was still holding my hand; I got out going back to the same old place,
But this time I hadn't forgotten God's grace; I tried going back to my old habits in which it just wasn't the same. I was tired and I knew Instead on losing my life, I had one to gain.

I picked up the phone and called the angel God had sent me before, and before I knew it, God's crew was knocking at my door.

They were full of the spirit and had their battle gear ready to go, and all of a sudden a beautiful voice sang Praises to God with a heavenly flow.

The music began penetrating my heart with an agape love, filling my mind with a peace that I didn't want to cease, opening my ears so I can hear God's voice. A feeling in which I knew I could rejoice. The angels started to pray for me. Little by little they were setting me free.

Once they left to go home, again I felt alone.
I knew what I had felt was real, but I knew something was missing still.

I was tempted to go back to the old way; But God told me I needed somewhere else to stay.

I called the angel once again; I was waiting on her porch when she got in. My bags packed, holding them in my hand. I knew it was time for me to take a stand. Alone I've been ripped apart not able to hide from the enemy's dart. Now I know a good place to hide where I'm not alone, and everything that is good, I am shown. My focus will continue on the One who loved me enough to die, and everything the world tells me will not fly. I have the truth that knows lies within, and every time I think of my Father, all I can do is grin. Because in my heart I know the devil did not win.

BY: CASEY

Warrior

October is not just for costumes,
Carving pumpkins and trick or treat.
It is to represent the war, that you battled,
And now beat.
Over the years, I have lacked on giving you
The credit where it is due.
So I dedicate this to you, Mom…
For remaining strong
And staying true.
The years have come and gone now… and
The tables have finally turned
So much have you tried to teach me…
And I'm starting to finally learn.
Why did I take this fight?
To bring the darkness to light?
I will never forget this phone call, the fear inside
Your voice.
The cancer chose you, Mom; you didn't have a
choice.
You did it for Kaleb, for Grammie, Chris and me.
You did it for the ones in Heaven, that we feel but
cannot see.
Not once did you feel sorry for yourself, or play
The victim's dance.
The disease had no idea that it would never
Stand a chance.
Your strength runs in our blood,
Straight into our heart.
Right now just a few miles away
But we are worlds apart.
I pray for you daily, and ask God to hold

You tight.
If I turn out to be half the woman you are,
I know I will be all right.
So this goes out to the families, enduring the pain,
And who are unsure.
Find your inner Warrior…and together,
Let's fight for a cure.

Bonnie

You Are

You are my passion. You are my pain reliever. You are my heart. You are my mind. You are my Spirit.

The years when I was lost, You waited patiently. Whispering Your directions in my heart; knowing one day You would be heard and my flesh would be silenced.

When satan had me in his death grip, You used Your mighty power to tell him to go to hell!

You are my Father, my Protector in the dark times. Without You I wandered aimlessly trying to figure life out. With Your endless love, You told me that's not my job.

You are my Love, my Best Friend, the One I run to. You are trustworthy, the One I tell my secrets to even though You know them.

You are my laughter through the tears. You are the song I sing.

You are the reason I want to share my life's story with people who may not know how BEAUTIFUL YOU ARE!

----Jamielou

The following is actually a song that I read to the women in jail. The words are so powerful, and it really speaks to a lot of women.

The Secret Place

My heart is like a house,
One day I let the Savior in.
There are many rooms
Where we would visit now and then.
But then one day He saw that door,
I knew the day had come too soon.
I said Jesus I'm not ready for us to visit in that room.

That's a place in my heart,
Where even I don't go.
I have some things hidden there
I don't want no one to know.

But He handed me the key,
With tears of love on His face.
He said, "I want to set you free,
Please let me in your secret place."

So I opened up the door,
And as the two of us walked in,
I was so ashamed,

His light revealed my hidden sin.
But when I think about that room now,
I'm not ashamed anymore
'Cuz I know my hidden sin,
No longer hides behind that door.

That was a place in my heart
Where even I wouldn't go
I had some things hidden there
I didn't want no one to know.

But He handed me the key
With tears of love on His face
And He said I want to set you free
I let Him in my secret place.

Is there a place in your heart
Where even you don't go?
You have some things hidden there
That you don't want no one to know.

Well, He's handing you the key
With tears of love on His face.
Jesus wants to set you free,
Please let Him in your secret place.

By Michael Booth

Chapter 11
Letters from Family Friends & Volunteers

~~~~~~~~~~~~~~~~~~~~~~

Letter from Rocky

When I met Missy, we both knew it was not a coincidence. She knew nothing about divine meetings, and I had walked so far away from my Christian raising. I was only looking for the things that pleased my flesh.

However, each time my life fell apart, I would return to what I knew from my childhood as I recalled the countless hours my mother had read the Bible to me.

One night in grief prior to meeting Missy, I was calling out to the Lord about the mess I had made of my life when He showed me the silhouette of a small woman with long dark hair with two kids. I could not tell the gender of the two children. I was comforted in the fact that with all my failures, God had someone for me.

I cannot remember how much time went by before I met Missy, but I had forgotten about the vision.

Once Missy and I were dating, I did what I always did; I walked after my own fleshly desires. Our relationship roller coasted up and down with problems in areas we would not yield to each other or to God.

I remember once when we were broken up, I ran into her twice in the same day. It was too much for me, and I tried to see her that night after being apart for three months. She had begun to date someone else.

I realized so many things that night as I drove the hour's drive back to my hometown. At first I was mad, and I called her abusively on the phone even though I was the one who had broken off the relationship three months earlier.

Late that night, I began to feel ashamed of the way I had handled it, and I remembered the vision once again. I cried out to the Lord. I confessed my sins and tried to remind Him of the vision (Like HE might need to be reminded of the vision He gave me!).

I told the Lord I was done trying to do things in my own strength. I was simply letting it go. I put it all in His hands and walked away for good. I would try to get my own life right and would not worry about anyone else. I knew I wanted to marry a Christian woman, and I was not walking a Christian man's life. A peace came over me that I had never known before. It was so calming that I know I could live without anyone but God. The peace was so amazing; the hurt of seeing her with someone else was gone.

I told God that it must be someone else in the vision, so I would wait to meet her. The next morning, Missy and her oldest son came by the house. I was in shock because I had just told her the night before that I never wanted to see her again. I stood there and could not believe my ears as she told me she wanted us to try again. I told her that I did, too, but it had to be different. I wanted to try to live right.

This was a giant battle for me because at that time in her life, her outside beauty was what was only seen. We began to try different churches. We went to all of them within a fifty-mile circle of her hometown. We dated for months, and then decided we would get married.

I had not officially asked her to marry me, but I knew we were on the right road. One day I went to see her, and she told me that she had been to a Chonda Pierce concert with two of the ladies from work. At the concert, she had given her life to Christ and asked Him to be her Lord and Savior. I was glad. I had seen a lot of people do this, but later there was no evident change. But Missy was different. She could not put the Bible that I had bought for her down. She had questions I could not answer. She began growing from a flower into a tree. That Valentine's Day, I asked her to marry me. We were married five months later.

As she grew, God was working on cleaning up areas in me that I had struggled with since I was 15 years old. But her growth was so much faster, if I had not loved watching it in her, I would have become jealous. Once after watching her read and pray until three and four o'clock in the morning, I asked her about it. I actually remember her answer just like it was yesterday. She said, "I have had what the world has to offer, and I don't want that anymore. I only want what God has for me."

A change began again as she no longer wanted to work for name brand clothes or a nicer car. All she could talk about was helping battered women. We had started attending a small church that met in a cattle auction barn. When they announced that they needed volunteers for jail ministry, particularly the women's side, she signed us both up! It wasn't really my calling, and I was glad to help, but she had found hers. She literally stayed there for as long as they would let her.

The more God moved on the women, the more she wanted to be used by Him. She loved them all and began to know them personally. I remember the first time we met a lady on the street panhandling sex for drugs and she called out to Missy, "Hey, Miss Missy!" Missy went over to talk to her. Without thinking, I asked, "How do you know her?" She laughed and said, "She is one of my girls. She has fallen. She was doing so well, and now she is back in the same place as before when I met her. There has to be a safe place for these girls to go who REALLY want to change. Some place that people don't have to have money to get into or to stay. Some place the government doesn't run, just Jesus; where everything is about Him and them. There needs to be a place where if they want Him and want to change, they can stay."

That day, New Beginnings was born in her heart, and for the next six years she cried out to the Lord to open the doors. In His timing, He opened the first door.

Missy never looked back. It was so amazing. I worried about the bills knowing I could make enough for our house, food, clothes and bills, but wondering how I would cover two houses. I told her that I just couldn't see that we could afford to do this. She laughed and said, "We can't, but God can; and if He wants it, we will have it." She continued saying, "I don't know how long it will last, but today this is what I'm sure He wants; and when He doesn't, the season will change." I had heard of people charging Hell with only a bucket of ice water, but this was the first time I had seen it!

A close friend of mine who was retired from the Sheriff's Department told me my wife has the gift of faith. I really didn't know about that, I only knew she was dedicated to this because she believed God wanted it.

Missy was the same person in our home as she was in public, transparent and honest about where this was going. She knew God was on her side, and it was going to work because of Him, not her. We had seen miracles with our own finances, and she knew He would do it for one more house, a Christian safe house for ladies.

I was still crawling over my religious doctrine hurdles, and she was off and running. I remember once, she was outside singing in what I thought must be Chinese. When she came in the house, I asked her what she had been singing when she was outside? She answered that it was kind of like a prayer language. I asked if she was talking about tongues?

And I quickly told her all that died with the apostles. She said, "No, it didn't, and God gave me a song. Do you want to hear it?" Well, I was amazed.

It was long about this time that I kept having a reoccurring dream. The entire neighborhood was surrounded by a foreign military, and they were calling for Christians to step out. It was one of those where you are half asleep but still awake. I would hear God say, "Do you trust Me?" I could feel myself say yes. Then He would say, "Step out." I would say, "I can't. I have to stay here and protect her (Missy)." The dream would then be over, and I wouldn't think about it much. I thought each time I was doing right.

Then one early morning I had the dream again. I didn't know how many times I had had it, but this time I was awake enough to argue my case. When He said, "Do you trust Me?", I was ready. I said, "You know I do. You can have me to do what You will." Then He said, "Then why don't you trust me with her life?" I was stunned and almost ashamed I never saw it that way. I said, "I do, Lord," and I stepped out of the crowd and the dream ended. I woke up not realizing what had just happened until the first time Missy was out way too late and I began to worry. The dream then came back to me. I was wide-awake and saw it. There was no guarantee of her safety, only that I was supposed to trust and release her to Him.

People ask me all the time, how I can let her spend all that time with the girls and ministry. And I tell them that I was a bachelor so long that I really don't need anyone under my feet all the time, as I laugh. But if they push me, I tell them I could not face Jesus when He asks me why I stood in His way to use her.

I share all these private things not to build her up, but to let you know that what God has done for her, He will do for you if you trust Him completely.

Her Loving Husband and Brother in Christ,

Rocky

Letter from Becky

A mutual friend introduced me to Missy about 13 years ago. We had kids about the same age, and became instant friends. Missy was pretty new in her Christian walk and was just learning how to be led by the spirit. Little did I know, the Lord had great things in store for her. We started going to the jail once a week to do women's ministry. Missy had such a heart and burden for the ladies, she started going nearly everyday on her own. She would tell me that her heart broke for them when they got out of jail and had no safe place to go. She asked me to agree with her in prayer for God to supply a safe home for them. Before too long, she had invited one of the ladies to come stay with her at her house when she got out. We continued to pray for God to supply a home. Missy knew God was calling her to this ministry and took a huge step of faith by renting the first house, not knowing how she was going to pay the next month's rent or any of the utilities. She was relying totally on faith. I have seen her make many personal sacrifices to put the needs of the ladies before her own.

It has been an incredible experience to watch how God has supplied all the needs of the ministry through moving in the hearts of different people in the body of Christ to contribute to New Beginnings. There were many times it looked as though the funds were not going to come in, but just at the last minute, they always came through. I have been very blessed to get to watch God grow New Beginnings through

Missy's faithfulness and passion to be obedient to what He has called her to do. I have seen many lives transformed through this ministry. I never dreamed that New Beginnings would grow to include two transitional homes, eight apartments and three additional apartments. I am very thankful that I get to be a small part in such a wonderful ministry. New Beginnings is a very worthy organization to donate your time or money. It is totally Christ centered, and it is changing lives and restoring families.

Becky Jennings
Volunteers and Teaches Weekly Bible Study at New Beginnings, 2010 - present

Letter from Janet

My time with New Beginnings has been such a blessing to me. I have the privilege to see God at work in these women's lives every week. He has performed miracle after miracle. Not a week goes by that He doesn't draw us closer to Him through the work He is doing in all our hearts. From the new lady who just came to New Beginnings this week, to the ladies who have been here one or more years, He is Faithful to show us His Power through prayer and His Word in each life. I hope this book has blessed your heart as you have read what God has done, what He is doing, and we thank Him in advance for what He is going to do. The Power of this testimony is for His Glory.
I Thank God He led me to volunteer at New Beginnings.

My Blessing!
Janet Franklin
New Beginnings Volunteer & Prayer Partner, 2013 - present

Letter from Leigh

Everyone has a story, but most only want to tell the "happily ever after" parts of their lives to others. When I first met Missy, I was in awe at what an awesome single mom she was raising her two active sons. She always had them both dressed well and looking sharp. She also made sure they were both very active in sports, and she was their biggest cheerleader and fan, never missing a game!

What really amazed me was when I started seeing a change in Missy... a new boldness in Christ! When she was truly saved, she jumped in with both feet and never looked back! I would listen with amazment as she would share with me visions, dreams, and answered prayers.

Missy's heart to help women change their lives is obvious. She doesn't just give her time, she gives "her everything"! It is evident God's hand is on her life. She is totally obedient to Him. Her heart is not to boast about things she has done because she will always be the first to give all the credit and glory to God for what He has done through her. She realizes she is just a vessel used by Him to accomplish things for His kingdom and glory.

God has called Missy to write her life story in order to encourage others who have not had ideal pasts, and to let them know that their lives can be turned around, too. People who are struggling cannot relate to people who appear to have had only good times. It encourages them to know that others have suffered through some of the very same issues. It is not our human nature to be transparent with everyone about our pasts or mistakes we have made. We tend to want to hide those things, or "sweep them under a rug" so people will think we have always had it all together. Instead, Missy is obedient to God's calling her to share her story, the good and the bad, in order to help bring others to Him.

Growing up, God only gave me a brother, but He gave me the best brother, ever! While I wouldn't have traded him for anything, I still wanted a sister, too. God later brought me the best sister, also; He just gave her to me through my brother! I love Missy as if she were my sister from birth. She is a precious addition to our family!

Leigh Denard Little
New Beginnings Prayer Partner

Letter from Les Bruce
Former Taylor County Sheriff

I have known Rocky and Missy Denard through mutual friends for quite some time. In 2009, I became very close to Missy and her ideas that we both share which is jail ministry and the need for Life Skills classes to be created at the Taylor County Jail. Missy jumped at the opportunity and swiftly began her certification process. It was later in 2009, when Missy came to my office and shared some of her past weekend activities. At approximately 2:00am on that given Saturday night, she alone went to an unsavory portion of the Abilene, Texas community because she felt it was her calling to travel to this area because there could possibly be some people who needed her (God's) help. In the most professional way that I could conjure up, I basically scolded her pretty good and told her in no uncertain terms that she had no business there and how dangerous I perceived that to be. At that moment, I was introduced to the real Missy Denard. She allowed me to once again get a glimpse of God's face simply by saying, "Les, you're right. I have no business there, but God does." I then had a moment of heart check, and said to Missy, "I'll never argue with God." And I made a personal commitment of supporting God's work through Missy and Rocky Denard, true warriors of this community led by our Heavenly Father, Himself.

Les Bruce
Former Taylor County Sheriff

Strong Supporter of New Beginnings in various capacities, 2010 - present

Letter From Ms. Charlie

"What? Give up my Sunday School Class?" I had just left the class, and was walking down the hallway when I heard Him say, "I want you to give up your class." But God..."I want you to give up your class."

Give up teaching? I had been a Sunday School teacher for the last 50 years. I began teaching when I was sixteen. My husband and I had traveled in the military all over the world, and I taught everywhere we had lived. When we retired from the military, I continued to teach. Now He was asking me to quit! It was a part of my identity... part of who I *was*. I remembered the scripture that said, "The gifts and calling of God are irrevocable." What was going on?

Anyone who has tried to argue with the Lord knows that it is an exercise in futility. He is not going to change His mind. I could resist, throw a fit and be miserable, as well as ineffective; but He was not going to change His mind. Over the next few weeks, I was told to give up my job as a Realtor of fourteen years as well as my position as a life group leader of thirteen years. All the things that I had been "called" to do were now gone, and I was in a "holding pattern".

"Okay Lord, now what?" I asked. He replied, "Wait." "Lord, I am sixty-six years old. I don't have much time left." Again, I heard, "Wait." "But God, people will think I don't love You." Still He replied, "Wait."

My life that had been so full and busy seemed strangely without purpose. It became a time of searching the Word for an answer. I began to accept that my life belonged to Him regardless of what I *did*. It doesn't belong to what I want or to what other people *think* or even to time itself. He taught me to wait on Him expectantly; to gaze intently, watching for Him to drop the flag. There is a momentum that builds in the waiting to catapult us into His mission.

For the first time, I truly understood *Isaiah 40:31*

"Those that wait upon the Lord shall renew their strength,

They shall mount up with wings like eagles,

They shall run and not be weary, they shall walk and not faint."

As it so often happens, the answer came in a way that was totally unexpected. A dear friend, Marilyn Haley, invited me to go with her to observe a Bible class at the county jail. Rebel Taylor, another friend from our local church, was taking a group of ladies in lieu of joining the teaching team. At first I resisted. Why would I waste my time and talents on women who obviously were not interested in God? Besides, what if something happened, and there was a riot? I could be taken hostage, or even worse. If that happened, all the waiting I had done in the past year would be for nothing.

Everyone needs a friend like Marilyn. Her persistence finally wore me down. After all, I couldn't claim that I was too busy! Days of background checks came and went. Finally it was time to go. My apprehension grew as we were told to bring nothing but our driver's license and car keys. I remember taking off my wedding ring and replacing it with a cheap "look-alike." After giving my husband what I thought could be a real good-bye kiss, I was on my way. As I was driving, thoughts of disaster filled my head. Why did I say yes to this? It certainly did not fit my agenda… I had never even been in a jail before. God had big plans for me, and I was just getting off track. Little did I know how this night would affect the rest of my life!

Below is a copy of an email describing that night to a friend at church. I will let it tell the story.

Dear Beverly,

I am sending this note in response to our conversation last night about the jail ministry for the women prisoners.

Rebel Taylor had invited me and two other women to go with her as she ministers to the women at the county jail. With some reservation (I had never been inside a jail before) I accepted, knowing that God has been calling me to something new.

As we heard the doors lock behind us, the reality of another existence began to sink in. What if there is a riot and I never get out of here? What kind of people will these be? Thieves...drug dealers...prostitutes.... murderers?

When we got to the room, there were about 20 women sitting in a circle silently waiting for us. As I looked into their faces, I did not see a threat of violence, but a look of hopelessness and despair, a look of disappointment after disappointment.

We handed out the provided hymnals, and began with two old familiar hymns. To my surprise, the response was amazing! They sang like their life depended on it! (I wish our life group would sing like that). Rebel began to teach on wounds from our fathers or mothers that affect how we relate to God. I could tell that the message was getting through, as there was silent weeping from two or three in the room. A time of one-on-one ministry followed as we prayed with several of the women and heard their testimonies.

It was a night I will never forget! God shows up in the most unlikely places. Even prison walls cannot hold back His grace! It blessed my life more than I can say. I am so glad I crossed this line into "another world." Needless to say... I will be going back. I will never be the same.

Blessings, Charlie

This was it! I knew that I knew that I was supposed to work with these women!

It was not something that I had always wanted to do. It was not something I even had thought about doing, but THIS WAS IT! Rebel had mentioned a woman who had opened a transitional house for women coming out of the jail system. Her name was Missy Denard. I thought, perhaps she would have something that I could do. I arranged a meeting with her. At the meeting, we discussed all the details of New Beginnings, which was the name of her transitional house ministry. She told me her story, and I told her mine. We agreed to pray about my involvement, and to see what the Lord would say.

On a Thursday night in October, I began teaching a Bible class to the women at New Beginnings. We met every Thursday night, and I began to see the women change before my eyes. They not only learned how valuable they are, but they learned about a God who really loves them. They learned how to apply Bible truths to their daily lives. As I got to know them and they got to know me, we became a family. One night a week was just not enough.

I became involved with the everyday happenings and the ups and downs of their lives. We now have a deep love for each other, and I see them as my forever sisters in the Lord. I cannot imagine my life without them... their laughs, tears, hopes, dreams and prayers! They are, and will always be, part of my family. This has been one of the most rewarding things that God has ever called me to do! What a great and faithful God we serve! I will be forever grateful!!

"Oh, how great are God's riches and wisdom and knowledge! How impossible it is for us to understand His decisions and His ways!" Romans 11:33

Ms. Charlie
Volunteer at New Beginnings, 2011-2014

Letter from Timmy

Sometimes in our childhood, things happen to us that are beyond our control. These things affect us, and can do a lot of harm, as we become adults. We can choose to use this in a negative way, or in a positive way. Missy has been blessed with the gift to use all of the negative things that she has been through to help people deal with their past as well as to help them get through things they are currently experiencing. All she does is for the glory of God. It is never for selfish reasons.

It's not everyday that someone can say that his or her best friend and role model are the same person. I am blessed to be able to say that! God has blessed my little sister, Missy, with so much. In a world that sometimes seems bleak, she is my bright ray of hope. I thank Jesus that He died for our sins, and gave us a chance to be reborn through the cross.

I thank you, Missy for showing me a better way to live, and for never giving up on me when it seemed that everyone else did. I thank you for the friendship and bond that we have. And I thank you most of all for leading me to Jesus.

Ms. Wanda Murphree

"Out of Egypt in Modern Times"

In the Bible, there is an intriguing story of people entrapped in a land of suffering and sorrow. God chose a great man to lead them out of that harsh wilderness. As the story goes, the journey from Egypt to their Promised Land should have taken only eleven days, but because of their stubbornness, griping and complaining, it took a harsh 40 years! Most never made it.

God didn't plan it that way. These were His chosen people, and He had marvelous plans for them had they only been obedient.

Such is the story of a great modern day lady named Missy Denard, who also, out of obedience to the Holy Spirit, has led many ladies (over 75 of them) out of bondage into a meaningful life.

Missy experienced a drastic change in her own life when God saved her and baptized her with His Holy Spirit; she in turn, began to reach out to others who were experiencing their own "Egypt".

In the Taylor County Jail, Missy began teaching a lady's class of Life Skills based on the Bible. As their hearts were touched and warmed, many were saved, and some were even baptized right there in jail in a horse trough.

When they were ready to be released, there was nowhere to go in order to make the transition from bondage back towards a promised land. That's when Missy took action on a vision given to her from God. Due to her obedience, she was able to begin the first transitional house in April 2010. Here these women would have a place to live as Missy and volunteers continue to teach Bible Life Skills along with helping them deal with their many issues such as: how to trust and be trusted, how to love and be loved, how to be whole after being broken, how to deal with the many wounds they have experienced, and just how to be "normal". The end result being they would find jobs to support themselves and adapt back into society.

As in the Egypt story in the Bible, there are "bitter waters", but God promised in Exodus to send an angel to "keep them in the Way"...and to protect them.

The only obstacle then, and now, is the failure to stay on "the Way"....

One of Missy's girls made this statement: "Young women can read this book and learn from our mistakes; the mistakes that have taken us from our children and any dreams and the plans we had before."

That is our Dream!

Ms. Wanda Murphree
Volunteer at New Beginnings, 2011 - 2013
Prayer Partner, 2011 - present

Letter from Shirley

I met Missy a few years ago at a women's conference. I was impressed at the first meeting. God's love flows through her life in such overwhelming ways that even the most wounded heart can hope again. Over and over I have witnessed answers to prayer from small things to big things as women experienced a new beginning in a life of faith in a God who can do anything. There are so many things I could say about Missy and her husband, Rocky, and their family...but I just thank God for their example of a life of faith as God uses The Word through them and pours out to others. Such faithfulness to a great call! All to God's Glory!

Shirley Jackson
New Beginnings Volunteer & Prayer Partner, 2011 - present

Chapter 12
Call to Action

"Behold, I stand at the door, and knock: if any man hear My voice, and open the door, I will come into him, and will sup (dine, live) with him, and he with Me." Revelation 3:20 (KJV)

~~~~~~~~~~~~~~~~~~~~~

Jesus is the only one who knows how to heal every wound and mend all the broken pieces in our lives. Healing is a process; it doesn't happen overnight, so do not get discouraged. Keep pressing in and receive His unconditional love, and let His healing wash over you as you draw closer to Him. No matter what your past has been, there is a way to come through and be victorious instead of a victim of your past! Take God at His word and walk by faith. Listen to His voice and follow. You are worthy no matter what you have done or been through.

" If you confess with your mouth that Jesus is Lord and believe in your hear that God raised Him from the dead, you will be saved. For it is by believing in your heart that you are made right with God, and it is by confessing with your mouth that you are saved." Romans 10:9-10

You are more than a conqueror in Christ Jesus! You are worth it! Believe in who He has called you to be and know you were bought with a high price!

Epilogue

Epilogue

This book is written specifically for all the women who have been abused whether it was physical, sexual, mental or emotional. I would like to encourage you that no matter what you have been through, God will take everything bad that satan meant for harm in your life and turn it to good for His glory. We have to walk in forgiveness so we can be free of the bondage. Jesus came to set us free, so make sure you stay free and do not go back to living in the past hurts. You are very precious to the Lord, and He wants to pour out His unconditional love on you. Open your heart to receive it and don't be a product of your past, but be victorious in your future. You have a purpose and a strong voice to reach other hurting women. God will turn your pain into beauty. We do not have to know it all, we just have to know Him – Jesus! Never believe the lie that you are not good enough, because YOU ARE WORTHY TO BE LOVED!

Rocky & Missy

Missy is the Chaplain of the women at Taylor County Jail where she teaches Life Skills Classes twice a week. She is also very involved on a daily basis with the women who live in the New Beginnings houses.

Missy currently lives in Abilene with her husband, Rocky. They enjoy spending time together boating and fishing when they can find time to slip away. They have two sons who are both married and three granddaughters and one grandson. They also enjoy spending as much time as possible with their grandchildren.

www.newbeginningsbigcountry.com

A NEW **CREATION**

Missy Denard has been dedicating her life to prison, jail and rehabilitation ministry for women for thirteen years in Abilene, Texas. The Lord has placed a burden on her heart for these ladies who truly need the love of Jesus Christ.

As Founder and Executive Director of New Beginnings –Big Country, Missy started this transitional housing facility for women desiring to make a change in their lives upon getting out of prison and jail. New Beginnings homes have been transforming lives of women for almost five years now. They have helped over 160 ladies and have successfully transitioned many ladies back into society. Missy believes every lady who comes to New Beginnings is a success because they all leave with something they didn't have before they came. Seeds were planted, and they will one day bear fruit.

President of Goff Ministries, which is based out of Lubbock, Texas, Missy Denard has dedicated her life to being a servant of the Lord in many capacities. She continues to stand firm in the belief that all lives are worth saving and that Jesus Christ is the only way to complete and total freedom.

This book is based on the life story of Missy Denard who through Christ has been transformed from her past of abuse, dysfunction and pain into a new creation. God has given Missy a heart of love and compassion to help bring hope to broken and wounded women and to help them know the love of Jesus like they have never known love before.

Read more about Missy's Ministry
www.newbeginningsbigcountry.com

ISBN 978-1-940850-12-2

9 781940 850122 >

Cover Design: Carly Tobias